LUTON TRAMS

The Story of a Small System
1908 – 1932

Car No.9, travelling towards Dunstable Road, poses on Cheapside loop in George Street, in the early days – probably about 1908/9. Note the closely spaced overhead wires and the extravagant gas lamps outside the shops; these include M. Fleming's establishment, happy to sell you any artificial teeth you might require!

By
COLIN BROWN

CONTENTS

FOREWORD

Colin Brown's book has more than a little interest to me personally – firstly because anything related to trams stirs many nostalgic memories of riding trams in my home city of Birmingham as a youngster and secondly living in or near to Luton for the last forty or so years I have met many interesting local people with the same interest in tramways. I saw the original draft of this book many years ago when I first met Colin in Luton and after years of further research the original script has been considerably enlarged to cover extra details. The mass of facts, figures, photographs and drawings in the book provides ample evidence of the painstaking research undertaken with obvious enthusiasm by the author. The Tramways of Luton bring back vivid memories of the British tramway era – right back to that far-off day in 1908 when the first electric car entered service along Park Street.

Back to the present day and the activities guided by the Luton Museum, with the restoration of the only surviving Luton tramcar – No.6. Riding on the open top of this tramcar when fully restored, sometime in the not too-distant future is something to be looked forward to.
Peter Hammond, Caddington, Nr. Luton, Beds.

ABOUT THE AUTHOR

Apart from his interest in travel to far-flung places, in his retirement he is an Officer of the Light Rail Transit Association, advocating a return to modern Tramways and Light Rail, a member of the Tramway & Light Railway Society (South Beds. Modellers) and the London Underground Railway Society. Born in NE London in the mid-1920s and moving to Luton in 1949, he well remembers being taken by his parents most Saturdays by tram to local street markets. Most alarmingly he was on a London tram which made an emergency stop using its magnetic track brakes. As a result it left the rails and all the lights went out!

First published in the United Kingdom in 1999
by Irwell Press
59A, High Street, Clophill,
Bedfordshire MK45 4BE
Printed by DPI Printers, Luton, Beds

PREFACE

What follows is the result of some years of investigation and research and is pretty much complete. However, the author would greatly appreciate any additional information, corrections to the text, criticisms, photographs, tickets or other relevant items which may add to the knowledge of this small town system. Many people helped in the preparation of this narrative which is dedicated to June, my wife, a Lutonian who claimed 'I hate trams'. The following are acknowledged for their assistance:-

MR ALLEN, LUTON; BALFOUR, BEATTY & CO LTD Press & Publicity Dept, LONDON; ROGER BARTON, LUTON; TED BLACKBURN (One-time Motorman), LUTON; THOS G W BURLEY, LUTON; Late V E BURROWS, UPMINSTER; Late JIM DRANSFIELD (One-time Motorman), LUTON; CLARE FLECK ex-Archivist, LUTON MUSEUM; JOHN GILBERT, LUTON; GREAT BRITISH TRAMWAY NETWORKS', LRTL; PETER HAMMOND, CADDINGTON, LUTON; D W K JONES, REIGATE; LIGHT RAILWAY TRANSPORT LEAGUE (now ASSOCIATION); LUTON CENTRAL LIBRARY; LUTON MUSEUM & ART GALLERY, WARDOWN PARK; 'LUTON REPORTER'; 'LUTON NEWS'; 'LUTON VISTA'; Late STAN MORRIS, LUTON; A D PACKER, BROMLEY, KENT; Late R B PARR, BINGLEY, YORKS; ERNEST PRICE (One-time Motorman and Inspector), LUTON; ALEC SWAIN, FLITWICK; JOHN SAVAGE, LUTON; 'SATURDAY TELEGRAPH', LUTON; 'THE GOLDEN AGE OF TRAMWAYS', CHARLES KLAPPER; NATIONAL TRAMWAY MUSEUM, CRICH, DERBYSHIRE; 'TRAMWAY REVIEW', HISTORICAL JOURNAL OF LRTL (LRTA); MRS A L WILSCHER, WESTONING, BEDS (especially for valiantly typing from my manuscript); JOHN SHELBOURN (Transport Ticket Society) LUTON; GRAHAM SMITH (Beds/Herts Group Omnibus Society) LUTON.

CHRONOLOGY OF EVENTS

May	1900	Tramways first proposed
10 July	1901	Electricity Works opened
22 Oct	1901	Tramways Committee appointed
30 Nov	1901	Plans deposited for Luton, Dunstable & District Light Railways
5 Feb	1902	Light Railways Commissioners held enquiry
13 Jan	1903	Luton, Dunstable & District Light Railway scheme revived
18 May	1903	Borough Engineer produces plans for 4 miles of tramways
27 June	1903	Tenders put out for construction – none accepted
12 Nov	1904	Tramways Provisional Order applied for
11 Aug	1905	Order granted and confirmed in Parliament
Sept	1906	Overhead current collection decided upon
Jan	1907	Council decides on Standard gauge
19 March	1907	J G White & Co. Ltd offer to build, equip and run tramways accepted
May	1907	Council decided to allow Sunday trams
June	1907	1 year's extension of time for construction applied for
4 July	1907	Sanction by Board of Trade for £65,000 loan (27 years to repay)
July	1907	Council Seal affixed to draft Tramways Agreement
Sept	1907	Time for construction extended to 11 February 1908
7 Oct	1907	Construction started
15 Oct	1907	Contract signed
Early	1908	Electricity Works extended
14 Feb	1908	Trial of system
18 Feb	1908	Board of Trade inspection
21 Feb	1908	Tramways inaugurated
May	1909	Lease transferred to Balfour, Beatty & Co. Ltd
Aug	1909	Feeder bus service inaugurated to Leagrave
6 Feb	1911	Light Railway Commissioners hear application for Luton Light Railway
27 July	1911	Board of Trade suggests fitting of speed indicators
Early	1912	National Coal Strike affects tram service
Oct	1912	Lease extended for 10 years
28 Dec	1916	Worst accident occurs
July/Aug	1918	Two Sunday strikes
19 July	1919	Town Hall fire
		Cars overhauled and repainted
Feb	1921	Sunday services withdrawn
21 Feb	1923	Corporation takes over operation
21 May	1923	Ex-Glasgow horse car purchased
Feb	1925	Street market in Park Square ceases
May	1926	Some motormen and conductors join General Strike
30 June	1926	Borough Jubilee celebrations
	1928	Leagrave incorporated into Borough
June	1929	Brush top covers fitted to double deck cars 1, 2, 4 and 5
6 June	1929	First top-covered car used
End	1930	Eastern National offers to purchase system
20 Jan	1931	Eastern National offer accepted
12 May	1931	Minister of Transport rules against selling
28 Feb	1932	Last cars runs on Dunstable Road and Wardown routes
16 April	1932	Last car runs on Round Green route
Aug	1932	Track removed in George Street

INTRODUCTION

Situated as it is in a gap in the Chiltern Hills, some 30 miles north of London and near the source of the River Lea, Luton and its climate was ideal for its once-famous straw hat manufacturing. At one time, even the Police Force wore straw helmets in the warm weather. This industry, which virtually dominated the town in the 1900s, has now almost disappeared. The population when Edward VII came to the throne was 36,400 and it steadily rose to the 70,000 mark during the period of the trams.

Luton was a comparatively small place, with most of its population contained within a one mile radius of the Town Hall. Its development was inhibited, except on the north-west, by the surrounding hills until the mid-1920s. The town was proud of its electricity undertaking and boasted that its industrial expansion was achieved cleanly - without recourse to belching factory chimneys, by virtue of all the newly arrived industries taking cheap power from Luton's own electricity works. During the first decade

of the 20th century car, commercial vehicle, cooker, instrument, meter and ball bearing manufacture was established.

The electric tramway was rather late coming. In fact, subsequent to 1908, when the Luton tramway commenced, only three municipal and six company tramways were opened in Great Britain. The early years, from 1900 onwards, were to see the great days of the boom in electric tramways. Those first years – 1900 to 1910 – were something of a 'mini-mania', similar to the earlier

Kerbside double track in High Town Road, by Welbeck Street, before the Great War of 1914-1918. It is obvious from this view that the narrow streets of Luton were not really conducive to tram working at all. Yet there was little other traffic, as the roadway, casually occupied by pedestrians, demonstrates. Unwin's shop on the right is still a Newsagent's.

People crowd across the loop in Park Square and block the tracks in Park Street on the occasions of the 'Stattie' Fair, Easter 1927. 'Stattie' was Luton slang for 'Statute', which refers to a Bank holiday.

'Railway Mania' but on a much smaller scale. About sixty systems commenced operation in the first five years of the century. Indeed by 1914 there were about 13,000 trams working over 2,500 miles of route in Britain. During this 'mania' it became fashionable to have a tramway system, and no town of any size with any claim to civic grandeur considered itself complete without brightly-lit 'electric cars' threading their way through the narrow and often tortuous streets. In fact if the petrol-engined motor bus had appeared on the scene a little earlier it is doubtful if some of the smaller tramways like Luton's would ever have reached fruition.

Electric tramways reached their maximum extent in Britain (excluding Ireland, Isle of Man and Channel Islands) in 1927 when there were 14,481 trams operating over 2,554 route miles. Of this total 11,969 were municipal cars running on 1862 route miles of municipally owned, as opposed to private company track. In 1924 trams were running in 174 municipalities, but this figure had dropped to 160 in 1927. Company systems, which did not attract any form of civic subsidy, reached their maximum somewhat earlier, in 1920, when 74 systems had only 800 route miles, with a total of 2,850 trams. It should be noted however that companies enjoyed more running powers over municipal systems than vice-versa.

One of the first trams in Luton, however, owed nothing to the Corporation.

William Austin was a well known solicitor of the late 1800s and author of *the History of Luton*. He did not have enough land at his home in Cromwell Hill and had a plot in Clarendon Road laid out as a croquet lawn and tennis court. As a pavilion and summer house he had a London horse – or possibly – cable car, reputedly from the Old Kent Road line installed. A published photograph shows a party of about thirty Edwardian worthies and their ladies in 1906 grouped on and around this modified tram.

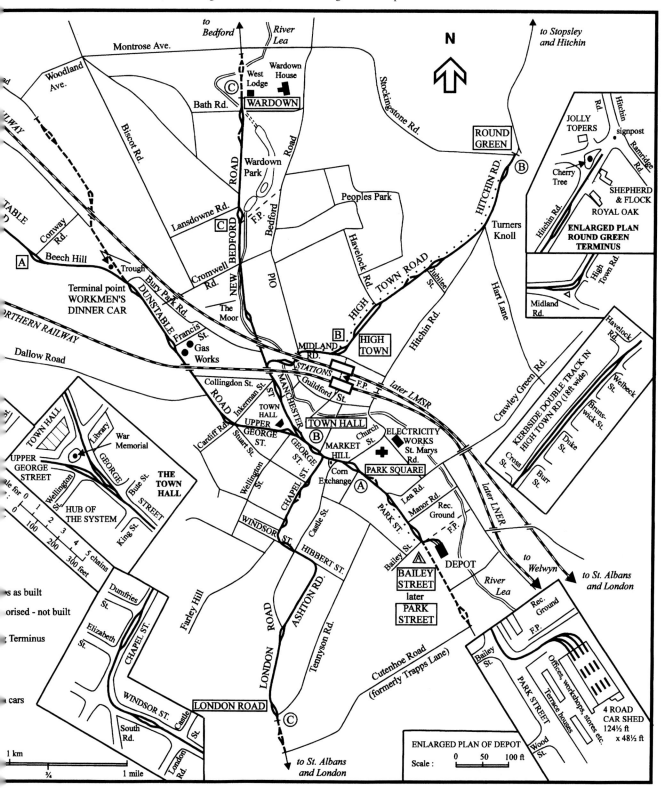

The Town Hall around 1910, with Car No.9 (the furthest one) entering the loop en route to Park Street. The Car on the loop is en route to Dunstable Road. Traffic as usual is sparse – only three horse-drawn vehicles.

CHAPTER 1

EARLY PROPOSALS 1900-1907

Luton, Dunstable & District Light Railway Plans resolved and question of current collection

Whilst a large number of electric tramways in this country were developed from steam or even horse drawn lines, Luton's system was proposed from the outset as an electric one. The first that the townspeople were to learn of these proposals came from a leading article in the 'Luton News' of Thursday 31 May 1900 which declared:
'*Tramways for Luton. That is the latest. Certain gentlemen in London are anxious for the privilege of providing the people of Luton*

that way could be satisfactorily overcome tramways would be a great acquisition and ought to do much to assist the development of the town. The council of course, will have to consider the question whether the scheme should be undertaken by themselves or left to private enterprise. Though there is much to be said in favour of the former and against the latter, the provision of a tramway system in a place like Luton is such a highly speculative business that the Corporation

Messrs. Walter Beer and Reynolds, Civil Engineers, of Westminster, to the joint Highways and Electric Light Committees. The proposal may well have been precipitated by the advent, in the forthcoming months, of the Council's own Electricity Works. Built in St Mary's Road on the site of the old Parish Church vicarage, it was opened on 10 July 1901 by Lord Kelvin. In support of the tramway proposals, Councillor Wilkinson had stated at an earlier meeting

The Luton town crest.

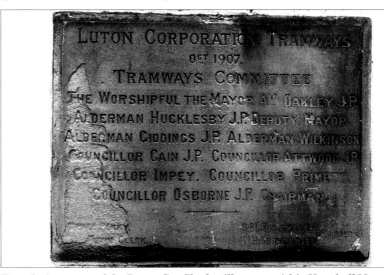

Foundation stone of the Depot Car Shed, still extant within Vauxhall Motors plant when photographed in 1984.

with a system of electric tramways and we are sure the people of Luton will be just as anxious to have their wants in this direction supplied.
'Unfortunately some of the streets of our town are very narrow and ill-adapted to a project of this kind, but if difficulties in

would be excused for hesitating before embarking on it.'

The proposals for an electric tramway system had been discussed at a meeting on Tuesday 29 May 1900 at the Town Hall and in line with the then forward-looking policy of the Town Council, a scheme was put forward by

that he '*did not know of a single Corporation running a tramway but what had made it pay after the first year of working*'. Prophetic words indeed!
Consideration of a tramway system was deferred owing to other important works which were on hand – probably the construction of the Electricity Works – until

The Old Vicarage, demolished in 1907 in a sad triumph of Mammon, to make way for an extension of the Corporation Electricity Works, so that extra power could be made for the new tramway.

The Curve under the Midland Railway bridge, at the junction of Midland Road and Old Bedford Road, under construction in 1908.

January 1901. At this time the question of the Corporation applying for a Provisional Order from the Board of Trade was discussed. Subsequently, at a meeting held in September by the Joint Committee, both Messrs. Beer & Reynolds and J.G. White & Co. Ltd. submitted proposals, but the whole question was further deferred. Finally the first Tramways Committee to be appointed was formed, under the Chairmanship of Alderman Giddings, JP, on 22 October 1901, for the consideration of any scheme, from any firm that wished to submit one, for tramways in Luton.

Plans were deposited at the Town Hall in Luton on 30 November 1901 on behalf of the Promoters, John Fell, Walter James Kershaw and Charles Osborn, by their Parliamentary Agents, William Webb & Co. of 37/39 Essex Street, Strand, London for the proposed ten miles long standard gauge

Luton, Dunstable and District Light Railways Scheme, in accordance with the provisions of the 1896 Light Railway Act. This catered for about five miles of line in the Borough of Luton with one route continuing on through the neighbouring town of Dunstable to the nearby village of Houghton Regis. The motive power proposed was to be electricity applied according to a system to be approved by the Board of Trade and supplemented if necessary by animal power or any other mechanical means.

A generating station, sidings, carriage sheds and other works were proposed on about three acres of land situated on the west of Leagrave Road in Luton and to the south-west of and adjoining the Midland Railway. The proposed lines were intended to be built along streets or on waste land by the side of roads. No land was to be acquired however, and way-leaves were to

be granted to the promoters. The engineers were Pritchard Green & Co. of 37 Waterloo Street, Birmingham and the scheme was estimated to cost £78,608.17.6d.

In January 1902 at a meeting held by Luton Town Council to discuss the Light Railway proposals, most of the talk hinged on whether the company would agree to purchase their traction current from Luton Corporation. Apart from the route to Dunstable and Houghton Regis, it was intended to serve the Round Green District of Luton from the Town Hall. A north to south line was also proposed, from the Borough boundary in New Bedford Road through George Street and Park Street to the bottom of New Trapps Lane (now Cutenhoe Road). Both these routes required the lowering of the road under the two railway bridges and this caused much concern and discussion with regard to the possibilities of flooding. As a result of these objections Councillor Gale suggested a rather devious alternative, from New Bedford Road by way of Cromwell Hill, Old Bedford Road, North Street, Havelock Road, High Town Road, Midland Road, Crescent Road and Lea Road in order to reach Park Street. This would certainly have avoided passing under the railway lines, the risk of flooding and obviated the need for lowering the roadways, but it completely bypassed the town centre and would have added about ¾ of a mile to the route. The outcome of the three hour long meeting was that the Council resolved to oppose the application for the Light Railway and make their own application for laying down, completing and working a system of tramways. Flooding still occurs by the railway bridges, even in the 1990s!

After this set-back for the promoters, they were approached by the Town Council at the end of the month in an effort to resolve the differences between them. It was pointed out that there was no provision for a service in the then populous south-western area of the town. The promoters agreed to take steps to apply for permission to serve the district in question as soon as consent was received for the original proposals. It was too late to include in the existing application and a further one would have to be submitted. On the question of lowering the road under the bridges, the promoters agreed to run single deck trams and thereby overcome that particular problem. In this connection the Town Clerk was instructed to write to the promoters and suggest that a shelter be erected in the vicinity of the Town Hall for the convenience of passengers who would of necessity have to change cars there; presumably to double-deckers. The need for the widening of the road between George Street and Park Square was put to the promoters and they agreed to undertake this work. All plans would have to be submitted to the Town Council for approval and an agreement would be entered into to last for a period of 35 years. The Corporation were still insistent that they should supply some of the traction current, even though the promoters intended providing a generating station of their own. Regarding the question of making good the road surface along the tracks, it was agreed that wood blocks would

Construction of the Car Shed in Park Street, opposite Bailey Street. View is looking north.

Installing one of the Town Hall loops, 1907-08.

be used in George Street, but the promoters were of the opinion that tarmacadam would be more suitable on inclines. It was resolved that the Tramways Committee should approve an agreement with the promoters and that the Town Clerk should attend the subsequent enquiry to be held by the Light Railway Commissioners.

Luton Town Hall was the venue for the enquiry which opened on Wednesday morning 5 February 1902 with Lord Jersey, on behalf of the Light Railway Commissioners, in the chair. The Light Railways Commissioners, set up after the implementation of the Light Railways Act of 1896, at the start consisted of the following members:- The Earl of Jersey as chairman, Colonel George Otley Boughey and Henry Allan Steward, and their headquarters was at 54 Parliament Street, London SW1.

The original intention of the Light Railways Act was to encourage rural development through the use of light railways. However, as a light railway was not defined in the Act, it was also used as a quick and cheap means of obtaining authority for street tramways. Light railways, moreover, only had to pay one quarter of their annual rateable value. After about 1899 the Commissioners would not accept applications for street tramways which were located wholly in one Borough.

The preamble stated that the ten mile long standard gauge line would be supplied with electricity by the overhead trolley method and would serve a population of about 45,000. Two of the arguments put forward in favour of the line were that the company would run workmen's cars up to 8am and also from 5pm to 8pm at ½d per

mile but with a minimum fare of 1d and that it would carry Luton pleasure seekers to the Dunstable Downs in the summer months (in spite of the fact that the tracks avoided the Downs by about one mile).

Opposition was forthcoming from the Great Northern Railway only 24 hours before the hearing, in spite of the fact that the notice of the application had been given 2½ months previously. The GNR's objection concerned only the section of the proposed line which paralleled its own branch from Dunstable North to Luton. Its representative stated that they had no objection to the Light Railway in the Borough of Luton or from Houghton Regis to Dunstable!

The appellants stated that the whole scheme would founder without the essential centre portion and that their line was not a real competitor with the railway as there was no intermediate railway station between Dunstable and Luton and their scheme was designed to pick up traffic from the north of the GNR branch. In support of the scheme, it was also stated that the GNR was not much concerned with increasing the traffic on their line, as they had been approached on a number of occasions to double the tracks and had refused. Although now disused, it is still mostly single.

The surveying of the whole route of the proposed Light Railway had been undertaken by Mr Robert Green, AMICE of Birmingham and Westminster. In reply to doubts about the suitability of the width of some of the roads in Luton, it was stated that, where a road was less than 23 feet, it would be widened to that dimension. The maximum width of the cars would be 6ft 6ins thereby leaving 16ft 6ins of space for other traffic.

The question of the narrow 18ft High Town Road was raised; the solution proposed was that a single track should be laid alongside one kerb, leaving a clear space of 10ft 3ins. In further support of the Light Railway it was pointed out that the cost would be £7,800 per mile, whereas when the Luton – Dunstable section of the GNR was constructed it cost £24,000 per mile.

For the GNR it was shown that they operated 214 trains per week between Luton and Dunstable, some of which continued through to Hatfield or London and that there was little need for any intermediate stations as there was 'not a half a dozen houses' on the main road in the 4½ miles between the towns of Luton and Dunstable. Despite this, after hearing the evidence from both sides and in view of the competition with the existing branch railway line, the Light Railway Commissioners ruled that they could not recommend an order in favour of the Light Railway. Its promoters again approached Luton Town Council at the end of February, but were told that, as the conditions had altered considerably, the Council could not give their consent to the part of the scheme as it affected Luton.

The tramway question was again raised at Luton Town Council meeting on 13 January, when it was learned that the Company intended depositing a further Bill in the 1903 Session. One speaker could not believe that a town with a population of 36,000 could support a tramways system and make it pay. 'In 20 years it might be the right thing to do' he stated. His opponents countered with the thought that if they did not support the Company now it would be throwing away the chance of tramways in the town for at least ten or twelve years. It was pointed out that the Company had agreed to amend the terms of the Agreement to a period of 30 years, but the Corporation were in favour of having this further reduced to 25 years. Alderman Hucklesby added that the promoters had still not made provision for the south-western side of the town and if they withdrew their bill for twelve months and then included this area, all well and good.

On a point of population. Luton was 75th in the country and of the 74 towns that were larger, 73 of them (and many smaller towns also) either had trams already or tramway schemes were proposed. Luton could not afford to wait ten years: *'If Luton was established, by the Company, as the centre of a large service from Dunstable and all the way to Harpenden and so on, they knew eventually that all the rural districts in the county would be laced by a network of tramways and the sooner the better'.* In spite of these favourable arguments the meeting decided by 14 votes to 9 to oppose the submission of a bill by the Company.

As a result of Luton's decision to oppose the proposed tramways, strong language was used at a Dunstable Town Council meeting on the following Friday. Dunstable had proposed certain amendments in the interest of the people of their town and had a meeting arranged for the previous Wednesday at 3 o'clock. However on the morning in question, it was cancelled on the receipt of a telegram from the Company, as a result of Luton's opposition. In a letter to the Town Council, the Chairman of Dunstable's Tramways Committee, Councillor Garrett, said that *'owing to*

Luton's selfish and 'dog-in-the-manger' policy, they have rendered trams an impossibility in the neighbourhood for some years to come, for if the present scheme is impracticable and unlikely to pay for some time, then any idea of trams for Luton alone being a financial success must be visionary'. The hopes and visions of tramways between Luton, Dunstable and Houghton Regis had twice been dashed in the past 15 months, firstly by the Great Northern and then by the Luton Corporation and they were between the 'devil and the deep blue sea'. It was suggested that Luton be told that their action was deeply regretted. The opinion of some members was that the hat manufacturers in George Street (Luton) were behind the move, as the constant flow of tramcars along the principal thoroughfare would interfere with the loading of hat boxes and trolleys.

Owing to the controversy over the tramways a letter from Councillor Albert Wilkinson was published in the *Luton News* on 22 January 1903 briefly reviewing the early history of the various proposals. He wrote: *'It was about 4 or 5 years since Luton was first interested in tramways. A year or so later Beer and Reynolds submitted plans from an engineering viewpoint, leaving the Corporation to finance the scheme. Nothing came of this; but subsequently, with the full approval of the Tramways Committee, a member approached the British Electric Traction Coy., who then visited Luton. However as they were fully committed at the time, the matter was dropped. Further to their visit, a Mr W Murphy*, who was the builder of the Ramsgate, Margate & Broadstairs tramway came and looked very favourably on Luton; but he eventually declined the*

commission. Next, Mr J Fell was interviewed, and he surveyed a route and proposed the Luton, Dunstable & District Light Railways, which as we have seen were successfully opposed by the GN Rly. The scheme was amended to suit Luton Tramways Committee but it did not cover the south-western area.

'We should look toward the future and learn from the past. The latest scheme could be advantageously enlarged to include the villages of Woodside and Slip End on the SW side of the town and north-eastwards to the community of Stopsley with a view to continuing on to Lilley, Offley and Hitchin – there being no rail connection of any sort between Luton and Hitchin. Such a network would be a boon to Luton's commercial prosperity. I do not look favourably on any scheme which is confined to the borough boundary, which would be a long time before becoming a paying proposition and not as useful as a largely extended system. A true assessment was required by a poll of the ratepayers'.

*William Martin Murphy of Bantry, S. Ireland who took over his father's building contracting business at the age of 19. He was a leading tramway builder in Dublin, Belfast, Cork, South London, Hastings, Bournemouth, Poole and Paisley and was also a director of the Central Tramways Company in Dublin.

It is an interesting fact that the 5 miles 2 furlongs Hitchin & Western Railway was promoted in 1889 to build a line westwards towards Luton via Great Offley, but strangely enough it would have terminated at Lilley! Had the business community in Luton been

Putting up the wires ('stringing') ready for the new tramway, with the aid of a horse-drawn tower wagon, Cheapside loop, 1908. Photograph Collection John Gilbert.

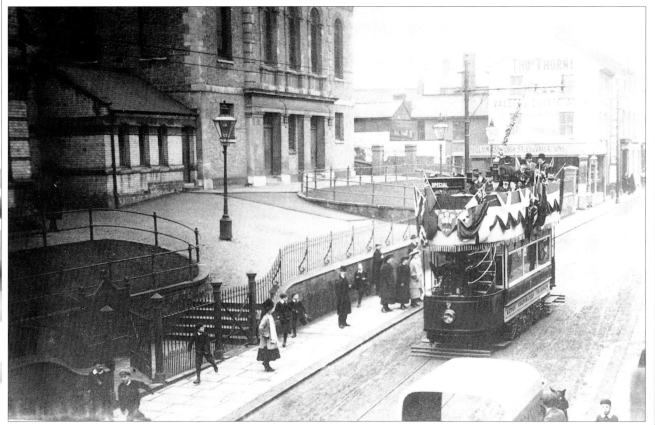

Playing its part in the opening festivities, decorated Car No.7, loaded with civic dignitaries, descends Chapel Street past the Wesleyan Mission on 21st February 1908. By a sad coincidence, this was also the last Car to work, on 16th April 1932.

prepared to raise the necessary finance it might well have reached Luton. Although the Bill passed through the House of Commons it failed in the Lords, and nothing further was heard of it.

Eventually, after all the discussions it was resolved at the Tuesday council meeting on 27 January 1903 that the Council apply to the Board of Trade for a Tramways Provisional Order. Subsequently, at a further meeting on 10 March, the Electrical Engineer was asked to submit a report to the joint Electricity and Tramways Committees, within one week, on the number of units the Electricity Works could produce in order to work 8 to 10 trams at a ten minute service. He was also asked to supply particulars of the cost involved and to state whether he considered any new plant would be required. After a lapse of two months the Borough Engineer (Mr A.J.L. Evans) produced a plan, on 18 May 1903, for four miles or so of tramways within the confines of the borough, at an estimated cost of £33,000. After considering this report, the Council resolved to put out tenders for offers for the construction, equipment and operation of the tramways, from company promoters or any other similarly qualified persons. Accordingly, an advertisement was published in the *Tramway and Railway World* of 27 June 1903; four different offers were forthcoming:

-William Griffiths & Co. Ltd, Hamilton House, Bishopsgate, London EC advocating their 'GB' (Griffiths-Bedell) surface contact system.
-Empire Electric Light & Power Co. (Dolter surface contact).

-Provincial Tramways Company. (Owners of the Stonehouse [Plymouth], Grimsby & Cleethorpes, Portsmouth & Horndean and Gosport & Fareham tramways Companies.).
-The Southern Counties Traction Syndicate (Electric buses).

For various reasons, none of the above offers was accepted. At about this time the Chairmanship of the Tramways Committee was relinquished in favour of Councillor C.H. Osborne JP.

The Southern Counties Traction Syndicate offer is interesting in view of the fact that they stated Luton's population at that time could not support a tramway system. Their proposals submitted on 30 July 1903 were for a system of 'electric buses' (what were later known as trolley buses or trackless trolleys) collecting their traction current from an overhead trolley wire, in a similar manner as trams. Their contention was that the system had all the advantages of tramways without the disadvantages of tearing up the streets to lay tracks. In their favour it was stated that it cost £5,000 per mile less to equip than tramways. Trams would not be a paying concern in Luton, they said, until the town was much larger and reached a population of 60-70,000.

When that figure was reached, it would only be necessary to lay the tram rails in the more populous districts at a relatively low cost, as all the poles, overhead trolley wires and traction equipment would already be in existence. The electric buses would run on the outskirts of the town as feeders to the trams. The system was already in use near Berlin, at Fontainbleau, Samois, Biela (near Dresden) and a bill had recently been passed

for its use in Stroud and at Cheltenham. The syndicate proposed five routes for Luton, all from the Town Hall; to London Road/Trapps Lane, Leagrave Marsh, New Bedford Road/Stockingstone Lane, Round Green and The Lodge (Luton Hoo). They also intimated that they would obtain powers to run to *Horton* Regis, Toddington, Dunstable, Eaton Bray, Leighton Buzzard, Slip End, Woodside, *Alley* Green, *Markgate*, Hemel *Hempstead*, Kings Langley and Watford. Not only was the syndicate highly ambitious but also a little unscholarly, as they should have at least studied a map of the district in order to give the correct rendering of names of the surrounding villages.

Mr William Griffith's offer was for constructing and equipping the system with the 'Griffiths-Bedell' surface contact method of current collection, after the Corporation had obtained the necessary Act. The Corporation was to supply the traction current at of 500/550 Volts DC and a cost of 1½d per unit. The contractor was not to sell the undertaking for 35 years. Apart from the expected routes from the town centre along New Bedford Road, Dunstable Road, Leagrave Road, Park Road (to Luton Hoo Park) and Round Green, there was one which was particularly interesting. This would have left town by Chapel Street and Farley Hill, continue along to Farley Green and into Luton Road to terminate in that road near the junction with Front Street in Slip End village. The Tramways Committee were given the opportunity of viewing the 'GB' contact system in operation at Ilford and it was agreed they should visit that town on 23 August 1903. The 'GB' demonstration line was located at the rear of the Manager's home and lasted from 1903 to 1908. It consisted of one-fifth of a mile of track, including curves and a gradient, laid in varying road surfaces. A single truck double deck car, with two 25 HP motors and Dick Kerr controllers, said to have been built for the Liverpool & Prescot Light Railway Co., was used.

All the members at the Town Council meeting of Friday 23 October 1903 and the various tramway promoters who had been approached, agreed that the routes mapped out by the Borough Engineer were the best and most likely to pay. Some discussion then ensued about the relative merits of the different forms of current collection. It was pointed out that the overhead trolley system was well tried, as well as being the most economic, effective and efficient, though the wires strung along the streets were unsightly to many people. The twelve miles of tramways in Wolverhampton were laid with the 'Lorain' system which, however, proved very expensive. The 'Dolter' surface contact system was mentioned as having been in operation in Paris, on the Bois de Boulogne, but as yet was unadopted and relatively unknown in Britain. Even so, the council at Torquay had passed a resolution to adopt that method of current collection.

The advantages put forward for the 'Dolter' system by Mr Slatter for the Empire Electric Light & Power Company were listed as follows:

It was the most simple of the various surface contact systems and as it had fewer parts than most it was much easier to maintain.
There was relatively little obstruction to the roadway as the contact studs were placed 15 feet apart.
The studs were very safe as the tram carried an earthing skate. In view of this they had a certificate from the French Government 'stating that no accident had occurred which could be attributed to their contact system'.
There was less noise with the stud contact system than with the trolley and that cars could pass from trolley to surface contact without stopping [but not the reverse!]
The studs could be installed at a depth of 18inches or as shallow as 11inches if necessary.
It had been in use for three years in Paris and was the only system which had the approval of the French Board of Trade.
The maintenance was not appreciably greater than the overhead trolley.
Dolter Electric Traction Ltd was an English company and all their equipment was manufactured in the British Isles. The construction costs of the 'Dolter' system were stated to be £10,000 per mile and the company were to be open to sell the undertaking after 10 years.
The National Electric Construction Company used the 'Dolter' system for the tramways at Torquay, Mexborough & Swinton and on the sea front section at Hastings, where it remained in use from 1904 until 1921.

Other places which eventually adopted the differing surface contact current collection systems were relatively few, but included Hastings, Lincoln, London (LCCT) and Mexborough in Britain and Monaco, Munich, Paris and Tours in Europe. Most of the various surface contact systems depended on some form of electromagnetic switch to raise and energise the contact studs and relied on gravity to return them to the 'dead' position. They proved to be rather erratic in operation and in most cases were unsuccessful, for they remained 'live' after the passage of the car, causing severe shocks and fatalities to animals and others. In fact in the LCC installation of the 'Griffiths-Bedell' system in Bow Road in East London between March and July 1908 when the cars were withdrawn, the contact studs had failed to operate on 927 occasions. Some of these were safe a short time after the cars had passed but even so seven accidents occurred for which the LCC was obliged to pay compensation.

After receiving reports of tramway inspections at Ilford and Ilkeston, the cost of which amounted to £10.13.6d, the Borough Surveyor suggested that the Council should lay the track and get someone to work the system. Consequently a resolution was passed as follows:- *'That application be made to the Board of Trade under the Tramways Act 1870, 33 and 34 Vic. Cap. 78 for a Provisional Order to construct tramways in the Borough of Luton'.* Alderman Oakley expressed the opinion that they would get better terms from the different tramway operating companies if they had an Order in their hands. He was rather frightened by the fact that a nearby town (Bedford?) had an order which was worth nothing because the electric lighting installation was such that they could not use the electricity for traction purposes. Things however were very different in Luton and this happy state of affairs had been brought about by caution on their part.

Board of Trade requirements included a minimum of 15 inches between passing cars, standards, curbs and so on, with span wires a minimum height of 16 feet. Rail weight was to be 90lb/yd but preferably 100lb/yd, car top deck rails to be at least 3ft.6in. high and the railgrooves not to exceed 1?in., though they could be 1¼in. on curves.

The regular Tuesday council meeting on 15 December 1903 heard, at an interview with the Permanent Secretary to the BOT, that Luton's application for a Provisional Order was just too late and therefore would not go before the Board until November 1904. Confirmation would thus not be given until July 1905. The meeting was advised

A Fair in Park Square with two cars on the loop, some time before 1914 – note the condition of the road surface.

More deserted streets. A Car (probably No.7) negotiates Ashton Road hill just above Cowper Street.

that if the Council thought it prudent to extend their scheme beyond the borough boundary and connect with one of the surrounding hamlets, they could then make an application under the Light Railways Act in May 1904. This would very probably be granted in the 1904 session and they would thereby benefit by having their tramways earlier. Three courses were open to the council to attain the goal of a complete system:
A Provisional Order under the Tramways Act.
An Order under the Light Railways Act.
An Act of Parliament.

In their parochial manner they decided on the Tramways Act Provisional Order. It was hoped to manage without agents, but in the event, Messrs. Sharpe, Parker, Pritchards, Barham & Lawford of Palace Chambers, 9 Bridge Street, Westminster were approached to act as Parliamentary Agents for Luton Corporation. The question of an alternative route by way of Castle Street was not entertained and it was decided to stick to the original route, up Chapel Street.

The scheme was considered practically complete by the time the council met on Tuesday 17 May 1904, in spite of some difficulty over High Town Road and

the advisability of using Wellington Street. High Town Road was said to be too narrow for two lines of tram tracks, as from the top of Midland Road to Havelock Road the width, in places, was below 18 feet (and still is!) but by interlacing the tracks and taking a strip of the path near the bridge the difficulty could be overcome, it was decided.

The busiest shopping street in the town at the beginning of the century was undoubtedly Wellington Street, but it too was only 18 feet in width (another one that is still unchanged 90 years later). It was also quite steep and some considered it inadvisable to take trams down such a steep

The 'Trough' (it was an ancient watering place for beasts on the road) at Leagrave Road, with a Car approaching from Dunstable Road terminus bound for the Town, about 1912. The Author used to live in the terraced house on the left-hand side of the photo.

Round Green terminus, probably 1908, with Car No.7 awaiting departure to Park Street. The rural life of course once touched everyone far more than it does now – Round Green with its sheep and farm carts was only a mile from Luton town centre...

gradient. To serve the western side of the borough, suggestions were forthcoming that the route should go along Stuart Street, the upper, less steep part of Wellington Street, Windsor Street and then join the Chapel Street section. The Tramway Committee decided that this would serve no useful purpose, nor could it make any recommendations regarding the use of Wellington Street. Later in the discussions Councillor Attwood supported the Wellington Street proposal, reminding the Committee that when a deputation visited Bournemouth, trams were using streets as narrow and very much steeper than the one in question. In Coventry, moreover, trams were negotiating gradients twice as steep as in Luton. Councillor Green, speaking on gradients, said he had seen trams in such Continental towns as Genoa, Marseilles and Milan going up hills compared with which Luton was 'on the level'. Even in small towns like Cannes, Mentone and San Remo trams negotiated steep narrow winding streets, which appeared to be extremely dangerous, without accident. The amendment in favour of using Wellington Street was carried with only one member voting against.

Two routes rivalled each other as the most suitable way of reaching the north-western part of the town. Considerable discussion took place on whether to use Leagrave Road to the borough boundary or the main Dunstable Road. The first named, it was observed, would bring the village of Leagrave within fifteen minutes of the Town Hall, but a disadvantage was that there were practically no houses along this road. As a result a route along Dunstable Road was

chosen. The committee were asked by Councillor Impey for an understanding that London Road would be linked with Park Street and Alderman Hucklesby said that unless they tapped the West Ward by traversing Windsor Street, Hibbert Street, Albert Road and thence to Park Street, the people of the borough would not be properly served.

On 28 June 1904 at the regular Tuesday Town Council meeting it was stated that Mr Crawley (a prominent local landowner) would be willing to give up land on either Dunstable Road or Leagrave Road for widening purposes, providing the Corporation erected a post and rail fence in lieu of the existing hedge. Although Dunstable Road had already been chosen for the route to the north-western area, the Borough Engineer was instructed to include Leagrave Road on the plans to be submitted. Further discussion ensued on the advisability of using Wellington Street, even though the Council could not see their way clear to having it included. It was stated that some shopkeepers wanted trams in their street, but the Council were equally divided, 9 for and 9 against, when it came to the vote, in spite of the fact that Chapel Street seemed the preferred option. Councillor Cain said that he believed that the inconvenience of trams in Wellington Street would be greater than their benefit.

At the following fortnightly meeting, the question of using Leagrave Road was again raised, when it was said that it would cost nothing to add it to the plans. Alderman Oakley said it was not the desire of the council to go outside the Borough boundary,

and that if the town were deviating in the direction of Leagrave Road then they might as well link Leagrave to the Bedford Road route; also, unless one were going to Dunstable the Dunstable Road route led 'to nowhere'. Councillor Horton stated that it would be a good thing if someday they could link Leagrave and Dunstable Roads by a tramway. He thought, however, that nothing should be included in the scheme that they didn't intend to carry out, and remarked that 'if all their ideas were included, they might soon get to Bedford'. Alderman Giddings hoped that the first extension would be in the East Ward.

At the 20 September council meeting a letter was read from Mr W. Crawley of Langley Street, saying that he wished the Council members could see the splendid motor buses in use at Hastings. He felt sure that if they did there would be no more talk about trams. The buses took their place with the other traffic and they could also take whatever route they liked. There was no expense incurred or inconvenience in cutting up streets to lay tracks. They had already been adopted by Eastbourne, where one bus travelled up a hill twice as long and as steep as that in London Road in Luton. It appears that Milnes-Daimler demonstrated a motorbus in Hastings, and the town was also visited by Eastbourne Council in early 1903 prior to their decision to commence bus operation in May. Hastings subsequently started tramway operation and had probably ceased bus operation by the date of the above letter, if they ever started in earnest.

CHAPTER 2
THE FINAL PLUNGE
Application to BOT
Construction, Inauguration and Official Inspection

An early view of tram ascending Upper George Street on a service from Park Street, alongside Christ Church.

It was reported by the Tramways Committee that the Borough Engineer, Mr A.J.L. Evans, CE had presented his plans and sections for some 6½ miles of tramways instead of the original 4 miles which they had approved. This was the final step before applying to the Board of Trade for a Provisional Order. The notice of the application to the BOT was made on 12 November 1904 and the proposals were for the construction and maintenance of seven tramways, wholly in the parish and Borough of Luton, as follows:

TRAMWAY NO 1
Single track with three passing loops wholly in Dunstable Road, commencing at the borough boundary just north-west of Arundel Road and terminating opposite Beech Road. Length including loops 8 furlongs 1.25 chains.

TRAMWAY NO 2
Single track with eleven passing loops commencing in Leagrave Road at the borough boundary about 2 chains south-west of Tudor Road, thence along Leagrave Road, Dunstable Road, Upper George Street, George Street, Market Hill, Park Square and Park Street to terminate in Park Road, opposite Trapps Lane (now Cutenhoe Road). 2 miles 4 furlongs 9.2 chains.

TRAMWAY NO 3
Commencing by a junction with tramway No.2 in George Street and proceeding northerly along Manchester Street and New Bedford Road to the borough boundary ½ chain south of Stockinghouse Lane (now Road) single track with six passing loops, one of them in Manchester Street being 5½ chains long. Length 1 mile 3 furlongs 8.5 chains.

TRAMWAY NO 4
Commencing by a junction with tramway No.3 in New Bedford Road thence along Mill Street, Old Bedford Road, Midland Road, High Town Road and Hitchin Road to terminate opposite the Wesleyan Chapel at Round Green. Single track with three loops and a length of 9½ chains of double track in High Town Road. (Note: there was to be no loop in Mill Street) Length 1 mile 3 furlongs.

TRAMWAY NO 5
Single track with five passing loops commencing by a junction with tramway No.2 opposite Cheapside thence up Chapel Street, Windsor Street, Hibbert Street, Ashton Road and London Road to terminate at the borough boundary opposite the upper end of Trapps Lane (now Cutenhoe Road). Length 1 mile and 1 furlong 8.7 chains.

TRAMWAY NO 6
Single track link line 1½ chains in length in front of the Town Hall connecting tramway No.2 and tramway No.3.

TRAMWAY NO 7
Single track link line at junction of New Bedford Road and Mill Street connecting tramway No.3 to tramway No.4 1.1 chains long.

Generally speaking the passing loops were three chains in length except where otherwise stated.

It was proposed that the tramways be constructed to a gauge of 3ft.6in. or such other gauge as might be determined – it was therefore not the intention that any form of railway vehicle should be run over the system. Provision was also made for operating the tramways by horse power or any mechanical means, and also by some combination thereof.

In the event only Tramway No.4 was built as authorised, the others all being shortened in some way, when laid down. Tramway No.1 did not actually commence at the borough boundary but slightly nearer the town at the 'Steam Laundry', at the top of Kingsway. Tramway No.2 did not traverse Leagrave Road at all but commenced at an 'end-on' junction with tramway No.1 in Dunstable Road at the 'Trough'. It terminated at the Depot in Park Street opposite Bailey Street, not as authorised at Trapps Lane (now Cutenhoe Road).

Tramway No.3 terminated short of the borough boundary at West Lodge, Wardown Park opposite Bath Road. Tramway No.5 finished short of the boundary, at Tennyson Road and the link Tramways Nos.6 and 7, which completed the triangles between two of the routes, were not constructed at all.

These Luton proposals probably came about in opposition to the resurgence of a line to Dunstable. This was a truncated scheme of autumn 1904, under the revised title of Luton & District Tramways. Due to objections raised about the narrowness of Church Street, the track was to have terminated in Dunstable opposite The Old Palace Lodge. Although promoted by the original company it is suspected that Dunstable Borough was behind the scheme. Bedfordshire County Council, though supporting the original proposal, was not pleased about the deletion of the line to Houghton Regis. The company, however, pressed on through 1905 with the prospect of a route to Leagrave; this was supported by Bedfordshire County Council in spite of the progress of Luton's application to the Board of Trade.

After serving Luton for nine years, from his appointment on 9 July 1895, Mr A.J.L. Evans, the Borough Surveyor, died at the early age of 41, on 13 December 1904, due to valvular disease of the heart. It was reported on 15 December that the Seal of the Council had been affixed to a long memorandum from the Mayor and Burgesses of Luton to the Board of Trade, setting forth the fact that the necessary advertisements had been published, and praying that the tramway order applied for might be granted.

Following expressions of regret on the death of the Borough Surveyor, the Tramway Committee resolved that the Borough Engineer should show a car shed on the plans, for housing the trams. It was to be sited at a very convenient point on a piece of ground attached to the Corporation's Sewage Works, and approached from Park Street. A suggestion that the Depot should be located at the Electricity Works was turned down as it would have meant opening a new tramway section (along Church Street) which was not shown on the original plans, and powers would not have been granted in that year. The estimate was discussed at length and finally approved.

After serving between 500 and 600 notices, the Council was pleased to report on 24 January 1905 that only ten objections had been received on or before 15 January, the closing date for objections. Small technical points were raised by the Luton Gas Co., Great Northern Railway, Midland Railway and Beds. County Council. Other objections were lodged by Boots the Chemists, Brown & Green Ltd, and four private persons. Objections from the Gas company concerned the possibility of damage

to its mains, due to the opening up of the streets. The two railway companies expressed concern for the safety of their telegraph and telephone wires where they passed above the tramway overhead lines. They required adequate assurance that the wires would be protected should they accidentally fall onto the overhead. The Tramway Committee agreed on 21 February 1905 that they should give both railway companies the benefit of all the Board of Trade stipulations with regard to protection of telegraph lines and erect a guard wire. They could go no further than that, and it was observed that they might have to fight these objections before the Board of Trade. In June it was learned that Leeds and Pudsey had also taken a stand against other objecting railway companies regarding telegraph wires, contending that the Board of Trade stipulations were sufficient. One railway company even went so far as to oppose the Leeds Bill on those grounds. It was pointed out that the Leeds and Luton cases were identical and therefore Luton would stand by any decision given in the case that Leeds intended to fight. The suggestion was made that Leeds, Pudsey and Luton should pay a proportional cost of the ensuing litigation. When the Leeds Bill passed through the House of Commons in July, the clause regarding the protection of the railway company's wires was deleted and it was therefore presumed that the same would apply to Luton.

Some people were still wary of the tramway scheme and its cost but they were reassured by the Council that the acquisition of a Provisional Order did not commit them to carry out the scheme; it simply made it possible. It was up to the Council to decide whether to go ahead or not, or to allow a company to start building. A 'Protesting Ratepayer' writing to the *Luton News* said

that £20,000 would be far better spent on rebuilding the Sewage Works and getting some pure air in the town rather than on a park (Wardown) two miles (sic) from the town centre or a tramway system, neither of which was needed.

At this time a large London company expressed a desire to run buses in the town. These were said to cost 14d per mile to operate – which was all very well for London, but not for Luton, where the tramways were expected to cost an average of only 7d per mile to run. It was observed that the bus would be 'the future means of loco-motion' and would be of great help to tramway systems, when they were stabilised to act as feeders from the surrounding villages!

On 21 February 1905, after interviewing a short list of candidates, Mr S.L.F. Fox of Newport Monmouthshire was appointed as the new Borough Surveyor, at a salary of £325 per annum. In his 32 years' experience he had been connected, amongst other things, with tramways costing £70,000 and also with the transporter bridge over the River Usk at Monmouth, a contract costing £80,000. A reminder of the early days of tramway promotion in the area occurred on 3 October 1905 when Mr George Sell sued Messrs. J. Fell, W.J. Kershaw and C. Osborn, promoters of the Luton, Dunstable & District Light Railways, for £52.10.0 which was balance of costs incurred by him in connection with their abortive scheme. The judge gave judgement for the amount claimed with costs against Mr Fell and Mr Kershaw, but dismissed the action against Mr Osborn.

As the running of a Municipal tram service was outside the normal function of a Borough, November 1904 saw the application in Parliament for a Tramways Provisional Order, at a cost of £539 – £290 of which was taken up in charges for the Parliamentary Agents. The Order was

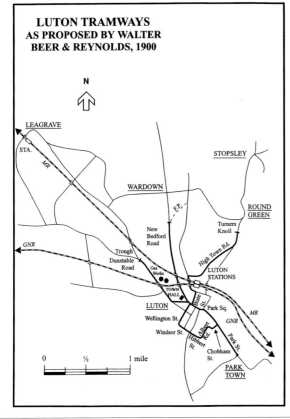

LUTON TRAMWAYS
AS PROPOSED BY WALTER
BEER & REYNOLDS, 1900

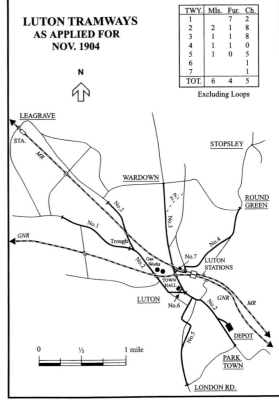

LUTON TRAMWAYS
AS APPLIED FOR
NOV. 1904

TWY.	Mls.	Fur.	Ch.
1		7	2
2	2	1	8
3	1	1	8
4	1	1	0
5	1	0	5
6			1
7			1
TOT.	6	4	5

Excluding Loops

An excellent view of the Carnegie Library with car No.7 passing en route to London Road. The Town Hall is out of view immediately to the right.

granted and confirmed in due course by an Act, the 'Luton Tramways Order Confirmation (No 2) Act 1905' which received the Royal Assent on 11 August 1905. The Borough Engineer, Mr S.F.L. Fox, was instructed by the Tramways Committee to submit a report on the implementation of the scheme in accordance with the terms of the Provisional Order. He was also asked to consider an abridged scheme along the lines of his predecessor's proposals of May 1903. On submission of this report, on 20 February 1906 the Committee recommended to the Council (by 7 votes to 2) that they apply for borrowing powers for £57,000 for the complete scheme. However, this proposal was referred back, by the Council, for further consideration on 27 February 1906. The beginning of March saw the residents and the Council alike still discussing whether to own and work the tramways or not, or whether indeed if buses would not be a better proposition.

Councillor Albert Wilkinson wrote: *'many ratepayers considered it would be far better for the Council to own and work the tramways and that they would be certain of ultimate profit'*! He also believed that motor buses were an advantage over horse buses which were shortly to be replaced in various parts of the country, but that they would never constitute serious competition to tramways... Tramways were *'certainly more expensive to lay down and equip but were very much cheaper to work'* he wrote. The seaside resort of Hastings had, until recently, run buses which it was now selling and replacing by electric tramways. He quoted the case of the tramways of Brighton where the population was 126,000 and the capital expenditure involved was £272,214. Traffic receipts amounted to £50,106 which yielded a gross profit of £11,829. The number of passengers carried the previous year totalled 11,321,160, which worked out at about eighty times the population of that town. Of the 54 towns of all sizes in the British Isles running tramway

systems, 36 of them made a net profit of £747,059 while half that number, that is 18, made a net loss of £39,740. Surely proof enough of the economy of tramways!

After talking for six years about tramways and trams versus buses, a new method of tramway control had appeared in the last 18 months. This was known as automatic regenerative control which was suited to more hilly districts. An advantage claimed for the system was that, the more hilly the district, the greater the saving of electrical power – as much as 25%. If there was still concern about the size of Luton being suitable for tramway operation, the case of Colchester was quoted. In February 1903 Colchester adopted a scheme of about five miles of route at a cost of £63,414 with a fleet of sixteen cars. Luton compared very favourably in size with Colchester where the expected loss on the tramways was equal to a 2d rate, although the actual profit amounted to £1,330. It is possible that Luton was compared to Colchester because that system was built by J.G. White & Co. Ltd.

The tramways of Ilkeston and Chester were both said to pay their way and it was suggested that, if Luton was too small to support a viable tramway system, why had the Council been approached by a variety of tramway operating companies? It was pointed out that though the Council was only applying for a loan of £57,000, it was not necessarily going to require it all. The Tramway Committee had a desire to start with only a modest £23,073 scheme for a line from Osborne Road in Park Street to West Lodge, Wardown Park and to the start of Leagrave Road, at the Trough. It was considered that a line from Park Street to Wardown might pay during the summer months, but also that it was the only route likely to make a profit. Consequently, at the Council meeting of 20 March 1906 the Mayor proposed that plans should be prepared for both Tramways Nos.2 and 3, as indicated in the Borough Engineer's report of 21

December 1905, also the short No.6 Tramway connecting the above two at the Town Hall. This proposal was carried by 6 votes to 1.

After a deputation from the Town Council had inspected the surface contact method of current collection in Lincoln and Wolverhampton and the overhead trolley system at Dartford, a report was submitted in September 1906 and it was decided to adopt overhead current collection. The Dartford tramways were operated, under a lease, by the firm of J.G. White & Co. Ltd of 9 Cloak Lane, Cannon Street, London. The Council considered this arrangement to be a good scheme and the Tramways Committee was authorised to enter into negotiations with that company with a view to obtaining an offer on similar lines to that with the Dartford Urban District Council.

In January 1907 the Town Council decided, on the recommendation of the Borough Engineer and Mr Beatty of J.G. White's, to apply to the Board of Trade for permission to widen the track gauge to the standard 4ft.8½in.. The narrower gauge of 3ft.6in., originally proposed in view of the narrowness of most of Luton's streets, would no doubt have been more appropriate, but it was rejected for reasons of safety. Various 'frontagers' objected ineffectually to the increase in track gauge on the grounds that it would reduce the space for wagons and drays collecting and delivering goods – particularly hat boxes – at their premises

On 19 March 1907, following a four hour debate, the Council decided by 13 votes to 8 to accept the offer of J.G. White & Co. Ltd to build, equip and lease the tramways for a period of either five or fifteen years, at the option of the Council. An amendment proposing that the Council should run the trams was defeated by 14 votes to 8. The terms of the offer were that the Council were to provide the capital required and that a rent equal to the interest and sinking fund charges would be paid by the Company during the term of the lease. Power would be supplied by the Council at 1½d per unit up to a quantity of 300,000 units, after which the cost would drop to 1d per unit. Fares were to be fixed at 1d from anywhere to the town centre. The Borough Engineer and the Borough Electrical Engineer (Mr W.H. Cooke) were appointed Joint Engineers for the implementation of the scheme. In May 1907 Mr J.W. Green, MP, wrote to the Council forwarding a resolution from a meeting of the electors of the North Ward, stating that no system of tramways would be satisfactory unless the workers received a minimum of 27/- per week and worked a maximum of 56 hours with one day's rest in every seven. The now defunct local newspaper *The Luton Reporter* carried a view of a proposed tramcar for the system, showing the destination 'SPECIAL CAR – CRAYFORD'; but with the words Luton Corporation Tramways superimposed on the rocker panels. It was in fact a photograph of a Dartford car operated by J.G. White.

In May the Council seriously debated the question of running Sunday trams. A controversy developed between the Mayor Alderman Oakley JP and the Rev. D. Caird

Looking down the narrow Wellington Street from Webdale's furnishing store, towards George Street and the Carnegie Library, with a Round Green tram on the Town Hall loop.

and after being strenuously opposed by the Luton Free Church and others, the Town Council determined, by only 11 votes to 9, in favour of running trams between the hours of 1pm and 10pm on the Sabbath. In June 1907 application was made to the Board of Trade for one year's extension of time within which to begin construction. Sanction was given by the Board of Trade on 4 July 1907 for the widening of the gauge and for a loan of £65,000 with a period of 27 years for repayment of the total amount. About this time the Seal of the Town Council was affixed to the draft Tramway Agreement with J.G. White & Co. Ltd.

Information was received in September from the Board of Trade, to the effect that the time limit for the 'substantial commencement' of the construction work had been extended to 11 February the following year. Construction was started in earnest and rails laid alongside Wardown Park on 7 October. A week later the contract for the system was signed.

In the early part of 1908 work was begun to extend the Electricity Works, in St Mary's Road, to cater for the extra equipment required for the supply of traction current to the tramways. The original equipment installed in 1901 for general lighting and power purposes consisted of three high-speed steam engines coupled to generators and one steam balancer supplied by W.H. Allen, Sons & Co. Ltd of Bedford, with a total capacity of 297kw. The engines were supplied from two 30ft x 8ft Lancashire boilers by Tinkers Ltd of Hyde, Cheshire in connection with a Green's economiser. Joseph Wright of Tipton, Staffs supplied the condensing plant. Mr Albion T. Snell was Consulting Engineer for this scheme, plus the distribution mains, the total cost of which was £25,000. Mr W.H. Cooke – the Electrical Engineer for the tramways, was resident engineer at the time.

An extra 30ft x 8ft Lancashire boiler equipped with mechanical stokers and a 350kw W.H. Allen engine and generator were installed towards the end of 1905 to meet increased demand for more electricity. For the tramways scheme an additional Battery Room had to be erected and a set of traction batteries with reversible booster and a traction switchboard installed. The batteries were supplied by the D P Battery Co. Ltd, Bakewell, the reversible booster was by the Lancashire Dynamo Motor Co. Ltd of Manchester and the switchboard was the work of Johnson & Phillips Ltd of Charlton, London.

In the event, after 'dilly-dallying' for over eight years, construction finally commenced, as stated previously, on 7 October 1907. By 10 October overhead standards had been installed all the way from the Depot to Wardown and the Council's Highways Department had made a start on altering gas and water mains and lowering the roadway under the two railway bridges in New Bedford Road, in order to obtain sufficient height clearance. The work of laying the track, building the Depot and installing loops and erecting the necessary side poles and span wires for the closely-space two-way overhead was completed over a period of 4½ months, well within the time stipulated in the contract. It also necessitated the closure of George Street for the whole of the month of November. The total capital cost for the 5¼ miles of route covered (about 6¼ miles of single track) and twelve 4-wheel double-deck open tramcars was £63,000. The total mileage authorised by the Luton Corporation Tramways Order was 6½ miles.

The track, supplied by the North Eastern Steel Company, was laid in British Standard grooved girder rail of about 95lb per linear yard for the straight sections (BSS No 2) with an increase in weight to 101lb

per linear yard for the curves, which were to BSS No 2C. It was laid in 45ft. lengths on a bed of concrete 6in. thick. Continuous rail joints 24in. in length and weighing 100lb per pair, supplied by the Continuous Rail Joint Co. were used for connecting the rails. Anchor joints were not used; however intermediate anchors spaced at 15ft intervals were employed. Fishplates, where used, were only on special work. These were drilled with six holes to take 1in. diameter bolts. The points for the loops and so on were 12ft. in length, had 150ft. radius and were made in manganese steel. Automatic point shifters were not used. Crossings and points were supplied by Edgar Allen & Co. and special trackwork was constructed by J.G. White & Co. Soleplates of ¾in. thick rolled steel, supplied by Naylor Brothers, were used only at points and crossings. Electrical bonding of the rails was achieved with concealed bonds supplied by the Forest City Electric Co. and the track was cross-bonded every 80 yards.

Although generally speaking the inclinations were comparatively easy, there was a short length at 1 in 11.5. Generally the track was paved with granite setts, to the usual width of 18in. outside the running rails as required by law, but in George Street and also outside places of worship, Jarrah wood and creosoted deal blocks were used in an attempt to reduce noise; a not uncommon practice at that time. The overhead consisted of grooved copper trolley wire supplied by W.J. Dennis & Co., suspended from flexible supports of galvanised mild steel wire stretched between doubly insulated globe strainers. Mechanical 'ears', manufactured in gunmetal, were supplied by the Electric Tramway Equipment Co. They were mostly 6in. long but in some instances ears of 14in. and 18in. were used. Mechanical, diamond and open type frogs were also supplied by this same company, in cast bronze. The guard wire, in galvanised steel and earthed above, was supplied by F. Smith & Co. This was hung from arms which varied from 8ft to 16ft in length bracketed from British Standards side poles supplied by John Spencer Ltd of Wednesbury. These weighed between 700lb and 1,100lb each depending upon their location and were spaced at an average distance of 100 feet apart, except on curves. Every fifth pole was securely bonded to the rails. The angle between the pole and bracket arm was filled with decorative wrought iron scroll work in a typical Edwardian manner as can be seen in some of the photographs. The pole bases were supplied by William Boydell & Sons and the poles were topped with a ball and spike finial. In eleven cases wall rosettes were employed in place of poles and bracket arms, mainly in George St.

The firm of Estler Brothers was responsible for the feeder pillars and section boxes. The feeder pillars were equipped with two 300amp. quick-break knife switches, four 100amp. knife switches and lightning arrester, test and telephone terminals. These were all mounted on a marble slab polished on both sides. Two 100amp. quick-break knife switches were housed in the section boxes. Cables and feeders were supplied by Messrs. Henley's and totalled 1.17 miles in length, laid solid in wooden troughs. A horse-drawn 4-wheeled tower wagon was employed by the lessees for the stringing of the overhead.

At the Depot, the car shed was built by a local building contractor, Mr W.G. Dunham. The steel framed gable end building, which also had steel roof trusses, was faced with Luton Grey bricks. It was 121ft.6in. long and 48ft.6in. wide and could accommodate a total of sixteen cars on four roads, each of which had a pit for examination and maintenance. The pits did not run the full length of each track but were staggered, the shortest being nearest the north-east wall of the building. Attached to the car shed on the west side were the Tramway offices, the Engineer's and Manager's office, a stores and a repair shop. In the 7 February 1908 issue of *The Luton Reporter* there was an account of a discussion in the Tramway Committee regarding advertisements. J.W. Green, the Brewers, were greatly surprised that the Committee had resolved not to grant permission for the firm's advertisements on the cars, more specifically as they had not submitted the form in which the adverts would be drawn. Greens stated that advertisements from outside companies proclaiming their wines, spirits and beers had been accepted. They were entirely at a loss to understand why a local firm and large ratepayer should be denied what was permitted to others without first being granted the courtesy of an interview and the opportunity to explain their position. As a consequence they respectfully entered a strong protest against such treatment. It was pointed out that it would be far more reasonable to permit local firms to advertise rather than people from outside the town, who weren't ratepayers and had no interest whatsoever in the town. The Committee stated that there was a clause in the agreement with the Lessees that they

would not display adverts solely devoted to alcoholic matters and they had no knowledge of an outside advertiser. They therefore had no course but to refuse Green's request. The only advertisements received were from J.W. Green and if they wished to advertise Mineral Waters and Ale they would be accepted. Mr Impey put forward the suggestion that the Committee should approve all advertisements in future before fitting any to the cars.

Local businesses 'jumped on the band-wagon' before the opening of the tramways. Henry Gibbons & Sons of Denmark House had an advert in the 14 February *Luton Reporter*, announcing: *'The New Trams start running on the 21st – our Great Sale is running now but will close on Monday the 17th'*. Another on the 21 February declared *'Trams run direct to the Luton Fashion Centre'*. A well-known provisions merchant had a map of the town centre with a location of its shop, affirming that *'Luton Tramways STOP at Inwoods Store for Best Value'*. At that time the shop was on the corner of Regent Street and Chapel Street.

Before the official opening of the system one car carried out trials, at 1am on 14 February 1908. It was observed by a very few late night revellers who solemnly declared they had seen more than one car. The single car journeyed to Wardown and back and afterwards made a return trip to Round Green. On board were Councillor C.H. Osborne, Mr Don (the Resident Engineer), Mr S.F.L. Fox (Borough Surveyor) Mr J. Ashurst (Assistant Borough Surveyor), Councillor A. Chapman, Inspector Franklin and employees of the operating company, Mr McInnes (General Manager), Mr W.H. Cooke AMIEE (Borough Electrical Engineer), J G White & Co.'s Superintendent Mr Bruce and the Chief Constable, D. Teale. The car was driven by Mr Sullivan of British

Thomson-Houston of Rugby; the firm had supplied the rolling stock, although construction was sub-contracted to United Electric Car Co. Ltd of Preston.

Two cars were in use on the following Saturday morning, when officials and employees of the operating company were passengers. Various irregularities in the track were ironed out and the points to the loops were being levelled by 'a smart little portable engine'. J.G. White & Co. had extensive experience in constructing and operating tramways and suggested to the Corporation that a public notice be prepared to warn all drivers of horse-drawn vehicles to be *'especially alert and to take care that their charges were not alarmed when the trams started running in earnest'*. The company in turn assured the Corporation that all Motormen had received *'specific instructions to assist those in charge of horses and other animals in every way'*.

The Luton Reporter carried a news item on 17 February 1908 describing a proposal to reserve certain trams in London for the exclusive use of women in the rush hours. This was due to the difficulties encountered by the 'fair sex' in boarding and obtaining seats on their journeys to and from work. The reporter queried *'will it be so for the 'straw girls' on the Luton trams when they commence operation?'* It is an interesting fact that special 'all female' cars were run between Port Glasgow and Greenock in about 1905, for the girls working in the Jute Mills. 'Ladies Only' cars were not really so unusual; they were operated for women war workers in 1916 for instance, by Newcastle Corporation along the Scotswood Road. (In fact it is known that Newcastle car No.102, now preserved by the Tramway Museum Society at Crich, was used on these duties).

Construction of the permanent way had been completed by 3 January 1908 and

The Electricity Generating station, built on site of the old Vicarage.

the Board of Trade was requested to carry out an inspection as soon as possible. The Inspecting Officers, Major J.W. Pringle RE and Mr A.P. Trotter arrived at Midland Road station at 10.44am on 18 February and after a short walk found a car conveniently waiting for them in Mill Street. This left almost immediately at 10.50, travelling up Midland Road towards Round Green. They returned to Mill Street and then went along New Bedford Road to the Wardown terminus. After returning to the Town Hall the Dunstable Road was the next destination, followed by the ascent of Chapel Street and Ashton Road to the London Road terminus. The car then returned to George Street, Park Street and so back to the Depot. Major Pringle's inspection was concerned with the tracks and their construction and Mr Trotter was responsible for the approval of electrical installation and the tramcars.

The Board of Trade report stated that there were a number of steep gradients on the system as follows:-

Dunstable Road route	1 in 15.7
Beech Hill	1 in 20.9
Upper George Street	
Round Green route	1 in 11.5 to 1 in 18)
Hitchin Road and	
High Town Road	1 in 12 to 1 in 16)
Midland Road	
Ldon Rd/Wardown Route	1 in 14.2 to 1 in 18)
London Road and Ashton Road	

Sharp curves were found at the following places:

Mill Street – New Bedford Road	40 feet radius
Mill Street – Guildford Street	42½ feet radius
George Street – Chapel Street	49 feet radius
Chapel Street – Windsor Street	48 feet radius
Hibbert Street – Ashton Road	36 feet radius

Speed limits of 4mph were imposed through all facing points (as was usual) on the curves between New Bedford Road/Mill Street, Mill Street/Guildford Street, Old Bedford Road/Midland Road and Midland Road/High Town Road, on the Round Green route. On the London Road/Wardown route between George Street/Chapel Street, Chapel Street/Windsor Street and Hibbert Street/Ashton Road. The same limit was also applied on the following hills: Hitchin Road, High Town Road, Midland Road, Beech Hill, London Road and Ashton Road. An easier limit of 6mph was permitted down Upper George Street.

On the comparatively level stretches of New Bedford Road, Dunstable Road between the Trough and the Gas Works and from Park Square to the Depot, 12mph was allowed. Elsewhere on the system 8mph was authorised. Compulsory (i.e. Board of Trade) stops were enforced at eight points on the system (see map) and the track brake was to be used on all gradients steeper than 1 in 15 and also before leaving five of the compulsory stops.

As many of the loops were not visible from each other the Inspector ordered that suitable signalling be provided. The loops in Dunstable Road between Conway Road and Beech Road, on the Round Green route between Midland Road and Mill Street, Hitchin Road and High Town Road and all loops between Windsor Street and Tennyson Road on the London Road route, were to be

so treated. If it was not the intention to provide signalling then evidence was required that cars would run to a specific timetable, thus avoiding the possibility of meeting between these points. However, when the system opened there was no timetable, the frequency being determined by the Duty Inspector. This haphazard arrangement was given as a cause for an operating loss during the first month of working. Subsequently a fixed timetable was implemented, involving a reduction in the number of cars operating.

The Inspector criticised the operation of the tramcar sandpipes; they ran from four sand boxes, one at each corner of the cars and, he considered, were too far forward of the wheels. This had the effect of depositing sand on the roadway and not on the rails on sharp curves, where it would be particularly needed.

The operating rods from the lifeguard gates to the trays also came in for comment, being some 3-4 inches too low for safety, as it was pointed out they would foul the ground on curves. If they were raised they would also be more effective, as the operation would be far quicker. It was also recommended that an oil lamp be carried on the forward platform of all cars in case of failure of the built-in electric headlight. Major Pringle also suggested that additional drain boxes for the track were necessary in one or two places in London Road. The Board required that the sandpipes were altered before public traffic began, while the lifeguards and the signalling was to be carried out within two months. The Board of Trade duly declared the system fit for public traffic and an order sanctioning the use of electric power was signed by Mr T.H.W. Selham, a Secretary to the Board, on the 21 February 1908.

Initially, at least, the driving staff were not recruited locally – the Board of Trade Inspectors had been informed that all motormen had been previously employed on other systems and they would be subject to one weeks' trial to learn all three routes. In fact even in mid-1907, before construction began, applicants were writing from such widely separated systems as the Chatham and District Light Railway and the Liverpool Overhead Railway, for positions as either motormen or conductors. It is probable however, that the conducting staff were drawn from the local district.

At the time of the inauguration of the system the Tramways Committee consisted of the following members:-
Chairman:
Councillor C H Osborne JP
His Worship the Mayor, Harry Arnold
Alderman Attwood JP
Alderman Oakley JP CA
Alderman Wilkinson (also c/man Electric Light & Power Comm)
Councillor Cain JP
Councillor Impey
Councillor Primett

The time and date fixed for the opening ceremony was 11.30am on Friday 21 February 1908, at the Depot. An invitation was duly sent to the Rt. Hon. David Lloyd George MP, in his capacity as President of

the Board of Trade, to perform this important function but he wrote to the Council on 31 January regretting that he was unable to attend. The Duke of Bedford, the next choice, was duly approached but he too could not attend and declined the invitation.

Next, two notable local dignitaries, Lord Ampthill and the Vice-Chairman of Bedfordshire County Council, Mr Howard Whitbread MP (of the famous brewing family) were approached and asked to jointly officiate. Luton was doubly unfortunate as although both accepted the invitation, on the day in question both these gentlemen had succumbed to influenza and it was left to Mr T. Gair Ashton MP (the Liberal MP for South Beds. who later became Lord Ashton of Hyde) to step into the breach. He also had a slight attack of the same malady, but delivered a speech from the platform of a gaily decorated car No.3 at the Bailey Street Depot. A telegram was received from Lord Ampthill with the message 'Best wishes for success of the opening ceremony and prosperity of the Tramways'. He also expressed his regrets at being unable to attend but said he was very ill.

The Light Railway and Tramway Journal requested information regarding the opening even though it was not included in the Press invited to the ceremony. There were 84 entries on the official guest list which included the Chairman and others of Dartford Tramways Committee and the Tramway Manager, Borough Engineer and Electrical Engineer of Northampton. The Press was represented by two national dailies, three local papers, three trade journals and, rather oddly, the Dundee Gazette. An eminent local photographer, Frederick Thuston, was authorised to take photographs of the ceremony and the guests at the luncheon held at the Town Hall. However, Mr T.G. Hobbs, another well-known Luton photographer, was not so lucky. He used photographs he took of the ceremony for 'unauthorised purposes' and the Town Clerk was obliged to write and ask him to withdraw some advertisements using these photographs.

The opening ceremony was acknowledged in at least three London national daily newspapers with The Daily Mail stating that 'all the equipment was of British manufacture'. The Daily Chronicle felt sure that before very long the Luton tramways would soon be linked up with nearby Dunstable, as did The Daily Telegraph.

It is not known whether Mr T. Gair Ashton joined in the subsequent tour of the complete system, on the procession of three trams. Prominent local personalities in the photograph of the inaugural car are, on the platform, the Mayor, Alderman Harry Arnold, with Mr T. Gair Ashton at the controls. Standing in front of the car are: from left to right – Councillor C.H. Osborne, JP (Chairman of the Tramways Committee); a tramways Inspector; Mr Bruce Penny, the Town Clerk and Dr Horace Sworder, the local Medical Officer of Health.

As the first car moved towards George Street at 11.45 one Councillor, who shall be nameless, was heard to remark that they would be going up Castle Street to

London Road. This was because he always went that way, in spite of the fact that the tracks had been laid in Chapel Street, to reach the London Road terminus.

The first car actually tackled the Round Green route, stopping on Midland Road hill to demonstrate the braking system. As they proceeded up the narrow High Town Road one wag was heard to comment: *'if you are late for business you could step straight out of your bedroom window on the top deck of a car, as they ran so close to the buildings'*. Because of the full load of guests and the brake demonstration the journey took a quarter of an hour. It was then a case of a return to town and a run up to the London Road terminus to complete the negotiation of the steeper gradients. Following the tour the assembled guests were treated to a luncheon in the Town Hall at 1pm.

The three cars, decorated with bunting, drapery, flags and fleurs de lys were particularly crowded with guests on the top decks at the start of the tour through the town centre. They soon relinquished their commanding positions for the interior of the saloons on reaching the higher, more windswept termini, such as London Road and Round Green. The usually jubilant crowds that lined the routes on such occasions as these were, in Luton, impassive and only mildly interested in their new transport system. No doubt many were slightly cynical of the whole undertaking after having waited so long for it to take shape. The tramcars, however, were very busy on the Saturday following the inauguration, being invaded as they were by many children spending their traditional 'Saturday penny', anxious to sample this new marvel of the age. Their

places were taken in the evening and on the following Sunday afternoon by many hundreds of their elders, also keen to try the new mode of transport.

Whether the Council could not decide on the form the bye-laws should take or if the question was just overlooked is uncertain. Whatever, in the event they were not published until 17 March and did not come into force until 20 May 1908. The penalty for the breach of any of the bye-laws and regulations was the general one of 'a sum not exceeding Forty Shillings'. The bye-laws were of the usual type regarding boarding and alighting, and smoking and so forth on the cars. The rear seats on the top deck were set aside for smokers. No standing was allowed on the cars (see later) except at the express permission of the conductor. 'Regulation No.6' also declared that when the car was full a notice should be displayed to this effect in a conspicuous position, but there is little evidence that this was ever done; in fact most photographs indicate tram loads were very light for most of the time.

By 28 April 1908 the Town Clerk had informed the Board of Trade that all the requirements stipulated at the inspection had been carried out except the question of signalling. This he referred immediately to J.G. White & Co. but the firm stated that there had been some delay in delivery of the apparatus. This may have been a device to disguise the reduction in frequency of the service as an economy measure. Mr W.H. Cooke, the electrical engineer informed the Town Clerk on 23 June 1908 that the apparatus had arrived and would be erected immediately, but there is no evidence that this was ever done.

Mr Trotter had pointed out that there were defects in the trolley standard leakage indicators on the cars and Mr Cooke had conducted several tests in order to overcome the problem. (Power was carried down through the trolley arm and the constant movement sometimes resulted in wear in the cable; current could 'leak' through the chafed part and cause a shock.) He had written to Mr Trotter on 20 April that the defects had finally been overcome, and had also told Mr McInnes, the General Manager, to use a particular type of fuse which had been found satisfactory. In an inspection on 20 June some cars were found that had not been fitted with trolley standard fuses to all indicators. Mr Cooke then wrote to J.G. White requesting that every car should be attended immediately. This was duly done and the Town Clerk wrote on 24 June to the Board of Trade confirming this action.

In mid-July the Board of Trade wrote to Luton Corporation reminding them that trolley standards should be electrically connected to the wheels of the cars in order to obviate the possibility of passengers sustaining electric shocks should the standard become live. The regulations stated that if the standard did become live the indicator should give a distinctive and continuous warning either by means of a red lamp or, preferably, with an audible signal.

No further mention of the signalling apparatus has been discovered and in view of the frequency of services operated it is assumed that the timetable was used as a means of regulating the crossing points on any particular route.

High times. Car No.4 about to leave Cheapside loop in George Street for Park Square, probably after the Corporation take-over of 1923.

CHAPTER 3
1908 ONWARDS

Day to day operation
Proposed Luton Light Railway
National Coal Strike (1912)

Cars 3 and 7 decorated and waiting to set off on their inaugural run over all three routes, 21st February 1908. This view is from a commercial postcard, posted less than a week later on the 26th. The publisher didn't waste any time in celebrating the great events!

The first few months of operation were not without incident, as a number of minor accidents and mishaps occurred. In spite of the public notice issued by the Council a horse bolted in George Street in March after being frightened by a tramcar. A policeman stopped it before it could suffer injury. An incident involving a horse and cart at the junction of Ashton Road and Hibbert Street in June resulted in the cart being smashed and the front lamp of the tramcar damaged. Again in June a man fell in front of a car in Manchester Street and a similar incident occurred at Wardown. Near the terminus in Dunstable Road a man was injured when he jumped off a moving car.

On 4 June a car left the rails on the loop opposite the Moor. This was caused by the motorman taking the right-hand side of the loop in order to avoid a horse which had fallen down across the other line of rails of the loop. About a week later at 7.15 in the morning a pony, frightened by a tram, bolted and the cart it was pulling struck a lamp post and was badly damaged. A couple of days later a car was derailed turning into Mill Street outside the Royal Hotel. This incident is said to have been caused by stones from road works, left on the rails. During the Whitsun Fair held in Wardown Park, extra cars were run and on subsequent fine afternoons a special car operated between the Town Hall and Wardown.

J.G. White & Co. held its AGM on 2 July 1908 when a dividend of 8 per cent was

declared for the year. There was a Reserve Fund of £80,000 plus accumulated profits of £16,249. The firm was originally at 22a College Hill, Cannon Street, London EC4 and subsequently at 9 Cloak Lane, Cannon Street. It was the British subsidiary of an American company whose interests in Britain comprised a number of engineering concerns. A civil engineering contractor, it built numerous tramway systems, but the only ventures into the field of operation were the leasing of the municipal systems of Luton and Dartford. Among others, J.G. White's construction contracts included the tramways of Auckland (New Zealand), Aberdeen, Belfast, Bombay, Bournemouth, Bexley Heath, Burnley, Colchester, Darlington, Swindon and Peterborough. The parent company in America owned several tramway companies in differing parts of the world, while the British firm managed two tramway undertakings in Brazil, the Paraguay Electric Railways & Lighting Co. Ltd, Paraguay and the Manaus Tramways & Light Co. Ltd, Amazona (reputedly the first electric tramway in South America) until at least 1939. Although the name of the company was changed in 1933 to White, Drummond & Co. Ltd it remained at the same offices in Cloak Lane.

The question of the difficulty in obtaining Workmen's tickets on certain cars was raised at a Council Meeting but it was pointed out that these services were marked in the timetable. Workmen's cars were run

between 6 and 8am but were not well patronised and were discontinued for a time.

People stopped the cars where they liked, and this drew some comments, to the effect that fixed stopping places should be designated. In fact, passengers waiting for a car were often ignored by the crews whilst people just standing admiring the trams were surprised to see one stop for them. Indeed some conductors had already been discharged for being impolite to the passengers and ignoring them. It was stated that notices and timetables should be fitted to poles at stopping places.

On Monday 6 July 1908 four cars were engaged under the direction of the Chief Inspector to convey children of the Wesleyan Chapel at Round Green on their Sunday School treat. The cars, decorated with bunting and flags, left at 12.40 for Stockwood Park, which was lent by Mr Francis Crawley. The return journey, again with the Chief Inspector in charge, commenced at 8.45pm after a very enjoyable outing.

The coming of the trams was certainly a good thing for some people, and it was reported at the Annual Licensing Meeting that it was a remarkable fact that there had been a big increase in the trade of the public houses in Round Green since the cars started running.

The performance of the tramways was considered at the Council Meeting on 7 July 1908. If they carried on at the present rate, it was calculated, 2,500,000 passengers would have been carried by the end of the year. The population about this time was about 42,000 and was to remain at this figure for two or three years. One of the Councillors said that the tramways were *'likely to be a little gold mine and the sooner the Corporation took them over the better'*. They were doing even better than Dartford, it seems, where J.G. White & Co. carried 40,000 per week in the first year. It was said a profit would be made if the receipts amounted to 8½d per car mile. J.G. White's working expenses were not known to the Council but costs averaged 5d per mile in Leeds, Leicester, Glasgow and Hull, the average receipts for those towns amounting to 10d per car mile. At this meeting it was decided to shelve the extension along Leagrave Road to the Borough Boundary for a further 12 months.

A procession through the town in mid-August in aid of the Luton Charities Fete assembled on Manor Road Recreation Ground where the entries were judged. The biggest show was made by the children from ten schools, carrying posies of wild flowers on a number of tramcars loaned for the occasion by Mr J.W. McInnes.

Ever since the overhead wires had been strung they had been a source of annoyance to the Midland Railway, because they were attached to troughs affixed under the railway company's bridges. A lot of correspondence had been entered into but eventually the Corporation agreed to the removal from the bridges. Standards were to be provided instead, supporting the troughs to which the wires were fixed.

The question of discipline among the employees arose about this time and in reply to a letter, Mr McInnes stated that there had recently been one serious breach of regulations when an employee had been given a week's suspension. 'Had it not been for the fact that he had recently married' he would have been dismissed. Another case occurred where a motorman stopped his car on a hill to take sweets from a lady-friend. For this silly and irresponsible action he was suspended from duty for two days.

A prominent London cycling journalist visited Luton in August where he 'found an unnecessary tramway and fled in haste and derision'. The Manager, on being asked for his comments replied 'cyclists don't like tramlines, perhaps he caught his wheels in the points'.

Up to this time there had been many complaints by the general public about gross over-crowding on the trams, with as many as 86 passengers noted on one car. The local newspapers took this up and asked the Corporation if they had forgotten the disasters at Swindon, Margate and Bournemouth. The latter accident had not been due however to overcrowding, which was not permitted in Bournemouth, but to an electric brake failure. Even so, seven persons had been killed and 26 injured.

The Council were approached at the beginning of October with a view to finding an alternative venue for the Fairs that were held in Park Square and Park Street every year in April and October. No solution was found and it was therefore agreed to approach the operators to start their services early in the morning and to terminate at the Park Square loop until 2pm. It was agreed that if it were necessary to get disabled cars back to the Depot this would have to be done under police supervision.

A novel use was made of a tramcar at the end of October when, owing to the inclement weather prevailing, a Coroner's Jury of 12 good men and true proceeded to Waldeck Road to view the body of a deceased inhabitant. The Coroner, who paid for all the return tickets 'hoped that the County Council would see their way clear to reimbursing him'.

The tramway company was sued for damages in mid-November when a lady passenger claimed that the car moved off before she was able to alight. The driver said he had stopped at Villa Road which was a 'request' stop and hadn't moved before she got off. The conductor was on the top deck, watching the trolley pole as the car passed under the low Midland Railway bridge. Judgement was found for the tramway company.

A letter in the *Luton Reporter* of 26 November noted the annoyance of the public who were being bundled off Wardown cars at the Cheapside loop so that the cars could change to the Dunstable Road route – to go for the football crowds and the quick profits. It was said that only one car had been running on the Wardown Route, instead of the usual three (?) for some time past. It seems all the profits were going to the company and not the Corporation and it 'was time they took the trams over'. It would seem that the published timetable was in fact frequently changed in order to clear any unexpected overcrowding that might possibly occur. Consequently the number of cars working any particular service could vary!

The number of employees at the end of December 1908 totalled 40 including depot and office staff. So that they could all attend their Recreation and Sick Club dinner it was held about midnight on Christmas Eve, in the staff mess at the Depot, after the last car had returned. The dinner was presided over by Mr McInnes supported by Councillor C.H. Osborne, Chairman of the Tramways Committee, who generously doubled the Christmas bonus the men had received from the company.

At the end of 1908 there was a prolonged snowstorm which lasted for 25 hours and produced the heaviest fall of snow in the town for 28 years, with 22°F of frost registered. At one time at the height of the storm the trams were the only vehicles moving on the streets of Luton. A snowplough of vee-shaped timber and steel was rigged up on the pilot board of one of

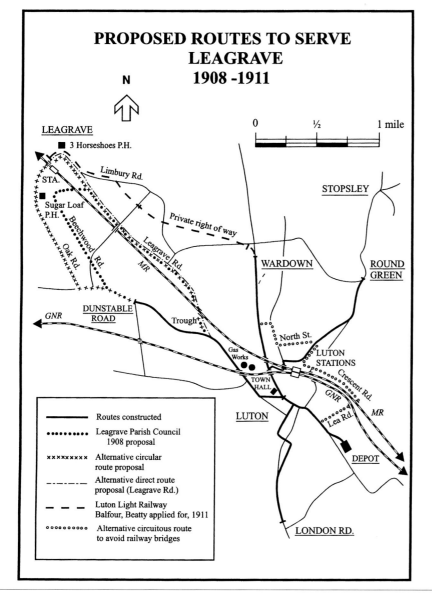

PROPOSED ROUTES TO SERVE LEAGRAVE 1908-1911

N

0   ½   1 mile

LEAGRAVE

■ 3 Horseshoes P.H.

Limbury Rd.

STA.

■ Sugar Loaf P.H.

Beechwood Rd.

Oak Rd.

Leagrave Rd.

MR

Private right of way

STOPSLEY

WARDOWN

ROUND GREEN

DUNSTABLE ROAD

GNR

Trough

North St.

Gas Works

LUTON STATIONS

TOWN HALL

Crescent Rd.

GNR

Lea Rd.

MR

LUTON

DEPOT

LONDON RD.

———	Routes constructed
••••••••	Leagrave Parish Council 1908 proposal
xxxxxxxx	Alternative circular route proposal
– – – – –	Alternative direct route proposal (Leagrave Rd.)
— — —	Luton Light Railway Balfour, Beatty applied for, 1911
○○○○○○○○○	Alternative circuitous route to avoid railway bridges

the cars and it managed to clear all three routes for a time. However, it was not very successful as it took service cars an hour to make the return trip to Round Green – a journey which usually occupied about 25 minutes. Eventually, after three cars had left the tracks due to the snow blocking the rail grooves, services on the Round Green and London Road/Wardown routes were suspended. One car only was running on Dunstable Road to the Trough. The snow-plough was out on the Round Green route on Tuesday/Wednesday night and did not in fact return to the Depot until Wednesday afternoon.

The question of tramwaymen's wages had been raised many times both in Council meetings and open letters to the local press. The Tramways Committee reported on 1 January 1909 that it was satisfied that wages were reasonable compared with other Municipalities; indeed, that they were up to and even above the average. The letter writers complained that the tramwaymen worked excessively long hours for very low wages, some men only getting 3½d per hour and that they were only supplied with half a uniform. Various rates were quoted ranging from 3½d to 5d per hour. One correspondent said they got 18/8d to 24/- for seven days whereas street sweepers received a guinea (21/-) for a six day week. Although the Council had no real jurisdiction over what J.G. White paid its men they were given every facility to inspect the company's books. It was discovered that a conductor's pay in fact was 4½d per hour and motormen were paid 5d per hour. Men new to the job received ½d per hour less for the first six months of employment. Conductors' wages in other towns were listed as a comparison:

Colchester 3¾d per hour rising to 4½d per hour after 4 years
Chesterfield 3½d per hour rising to 4½d per hour after 2 years
Yarmouth 4d per hour rising to 4½d per hour after 4 years
Ipswich 3d per hour rising to 4½d per hour after 4 years
Lowestoft 4½d per hour rising to 4¾d per hour after 3 years
Dover 3d per hour rising to 3½d

However, in both Doncaster and Southport, drivers were paid the 'princely' sum of 6¼d per hour after 'several' years. As will be seen from the above figures J.G. White was justified in its claim that they paid fair wages and that there had been no complaints from the men. Moreover, the Company were always receiving applications for vacancies, thereby proving the point that the pay was reasonable.

It was said that the tramways were not such a 'little gold mine' as was at first expected at the initial Council Meeting of 1909. The Company had reported a loss of £1,000 on the first year's operation. They had carried 2,131,635 passengers in the year and had traversed 279,102 car miles. This meant that the population of Luton had been carried 50 times over during the year. The people of the town had been told the tramways would be profitable if they carried them 33 times over. Now it was revealed that this referred only to the original smaller scheme of Mr Evans, with its proposed capital outlay of about £30,000. At about this time the Dunstable Road services were altered to start from Park Square so they could provide a 10 minute service instead of the previous 15 minutes interval. Round Green cars continued to work from the Depot and some consideration was given to the issue of transfer tickets for a change of car at the Town Hall. A letter in the *Luton Reporter* of 15 April 1909 again raised the question of

obtaining Workmen's Tickets on the cars. The writer suggested that the same timed car was for workmen on some days but not on others. He also enquired why women workers were not treated in the bye-laws as workmen.

Rumours of a transfer of the lease to another company had been rife for some time and on 4 May 1909 the Council debated the matter and eventually agreed to the transfer. On the formation of a new company by the Secretary, Mr Beatty and the Commercial Engineer Mr George Balfour of J.G. White & Co., the lease was transferred to Messrs. Balfour, Beatty & Co. Ltd of 22a College Hill, Cannon Street, London EC who took over J.G. White's responsibility with regard to the operation of both the Luton and Dartford tramways.

Digressing for a moment to consider the formation of the Company and the careers of the two Partners, in January 1909 A.H. Beatty, who was the Secretary of J.G. White & Co. and also a Director of two other tramway firms, joined with George Balfour to form the now very well known Balfour, Beatty & Co. Ltd. Mr Balfour had been a Director, along with Mr Beatty of the Mansfield tramways and was also a Director of the Dumbarton, Broughty Ferry and Fife Tramway companies. The new company was formed to carry on business as general and electrical engineers, contractors, operating managers for tramways, railways and lighting properties and for promotion of new enterprises. The share capital was £50,000 divided equally into ordinary and preference shares. The company started business on the basis of arrangements whereby Balfour, Beatty, in consideration of a payment to them of £5,000, took over J.G. White's responsibilities in regard to the operation of

A commercial postcard, showing Car No.10 in George Street. It was published in the *'Boots Cash Chemists "Pelham" Series'* and was posted on 18th June 1915.

the Dartford and Luton tramways. In February £2,000 of the money from White's was used to buy shares of the Cavehill & Whitewell Tramways Co. in Northern Ireland. This company had been incorporated in 1881 to build tramways in County Antrim and was later sold to Belfast Corporation in 1911, the arbitrator's award being £56,155. In March, Balfour, Beatty bought shares in the Mansfield & District Tramways from J.G. White. Mansfield tramways had been opened in 1905, was nine miles long and ran on electricity supplied by the Corporation. In May, George Balfour and A.H. Beatty together agreed to guarantee the bank overdraft of the Llanelli & District Electric Lighting Traction Company. 1914 saw a new subsidiary company, formed under the title of Cheltenham & District, to operate tramways in that area.

In the early years they shared offices with J.G. White in College Hill, but later on transferred to 66 Queen Street, London. They formed subsidiary companies, totalling eleven in all, from 1912 onwards, all with registered offices in Queen Street. As a result of tramway abandonment the firm was left mainly with electricity supply companies, which were all nationalised in 1947. Balfour, Beatty were still in business in the same area of London a few years ago with offices in Bread Street, off Cannon Street, as Electrical, Mechanical and Civil Engineering Contractors and there was still a Balfour on the Board in the person of Mr D.M. Balfour who was Managing Director. The whole of the share capital is currently held by Power Securities Corporation Ltd, itself a subsidiary of the giant British Insulated Callender's Cable Co. Ltd who have recently located all its offices in Thornton Heath, Surrey. They also hold, directly or through subsidiaries, the whole of the share capital of Balfour, Beatty Construction Ltd, Balfour, Beatty Power Consultants Canada Ltd, Balfour, Beatty (Overseas) Ltd, Balfour Beatty & Co. (Canada) Ltd and Balfour, Beatty Construction (Scotland) Ltd. So, from the small business which was formed in 1909 with a capital of £50,000, has grown a Group with total net assets in excess of £5,000,000. A.H. Beatty died in December 1934 and George Balfour died on 26 September 1941. A plaque was erected in 1954 at the North of Scotland Hydro-Electric Board's Tummel Bridge Power Station commemorating Balfour's service to electrical engineering with the words 'GEORGE BALFOUR 1872-1941 PIONEER OF HYDRO-ELECTRICAL DEVELOPMENT'. Balfour, Beatty were involved in the electrical work of the London end of the Bedford-Luton-St Pancras railway line and were also engaged on the electrification of the East Coast main line of British Rail, as well as Manchester Metrolink, South Yorkshire Supertram, many BR contracts and the Channel Tunnel. Balfour, Beatty are still very much in evidence in the Luton area, engaged in railway work.

GEORGE BALFOUR 1872-1941

George Balfour was born at Portsmouth on 30 November 1872. As J.G. White's Commercial Engineer he was responsible for Electric tramway construction at Southend-on-Sea, Shipley (Yorks) Clyde and Dundee. He was also on the board of tramway and electricity supply companies in Arbroath, Dundee, Dumbarton and Fife.

ANDREW HENRY BEATTY

Andrew Beatty worked in Newfoundland and southern Russia before becoming Secretary of J.G. White & Co. He was a trained Accountant, a member of the Court of Common Counsel, a City of London Liveryman of the Fruiterers Company and an officer in the City of London Special Police.

To continue the story:- it has been reported that a purpose-built horse bus plied on the Leagrave Road in 1901. This vehicle was owned by Mr Jabez 'Topper' Cain of Lilley and was stabled at Holly Tree Farm, Leagrave, and a Mr James Pollard may also have operated on this road. When Mr Cain's horses were requisitioned by the Army in August 1914 the bus was withdrawn and it was succeeded by a landaulette, owned by Mr William Burnage.

In view of the fact that no tramway had been built from the 'Trough' (for watering animals) along the important Leagrave Road, Balfour, Beatty commenced running a feeder service to the trams in mid-August 1909. It was operated by a solid-tyred, chain driven 18 seat single-deck 30/32hp Commercial Cars (Commer) motorbus (Regn. No.LM 8152) to the *Three Horseshoes* public house at Leagrave at a fare of 2d and the journey occupied a mere seven minutes. There was also a 3d fare issued on all cars from the Town Hall on the Dunstable Road route with a transfer to the bus at the 'Trough' for the journey to Leagrave.

Originally the service was every 30 minutes, but within a week it became hourly, although maintaining a 30 minute headway during the morning peak period. The bus was operated daily beyond the *Three Horseshoes* to terminate at another Leagrave pub, *The Sugar Loaf* where it was garaged in a barn. Although proving most unreliable at times, the service probably continued until March 1913. At one stage enquiries were made regarding the hiring of a larger 34 seat double deck Commer, probably from Commercial Car Hirers Ltd. It is believed that horse-drawn transport continued throughout the period over this route.

Eventually, when Balfour, Beatty gave up operation of the feeder service, Road Motors Ltd appeared on the scene, for about four months. They provided a generally similar timetable, although the first and last journeys originated at Luton Town Hall, due not doubt to the fact that the vehicles were kept in the yard of the *Horse & Jockey* in Manchester Street, opposite the Town Hall.

The running of the motor bus to Leagrave in conjunction with the trams caused more nuisance to the residents than they thought it was worth. In the summer it showered them with dust and in the bad weather its progress was likened more to a motor boat than a motor bus. In fact at times it sank so low into the ruts that it had to be dug out. The residents were against paying their rates until both Leagrave and Marsh Roads became properly made up thoroughfares.

A little girl had a narrow escape when she ran in front of tram No.6 in High Town Road about 10am on 30 December 1909. However the driver reacted very promptly and stopped the tram immediately. The child was found very frightened and upset but uninjured on the tray of the lifeguard, which had automatically dropped.

The construction of the complete tramways as authorised, was discussed at the Tuesday Council meeting on 4 January 1910. The decision was taken that the Leagrave Road section, the ends of Dunstable Road, New Bedford Road, Park Street and London Road routes and Tramways 6 and 7 should be completed and application would be made to the Board of Trade for a further two years' extension until 11 August 1912. However, nothing further was to come of this.

An accident occurred at 5pm on 6 January 1910 in Manchester Street which could have had serious consequences. A coal cart swerved towards oncoming car No.12, the driver Mr Maycock braked sharply but a collision was unavoidable. One shaft of the cart pierced the front panel of the tram just missing the driver and then crashed through the bulkhead into the passenger compartment. It was indeed fortunate that no one was occupying the seat at that point.

In 1910 the Coronation of King George V was celebrated with the cars decorated both inside and out. Red, white and blue drapes were hung in the saloon at the windows and the upper decks were encircled with red, white and blue bunting. A Union flag was carried on each side in the centre of the decency panels and the Royal cipher was prominently displayed on front and rear canopies. Pennants were hung from the upper deck floor and guard rails. They were also draped from grab rails and festooned the destination boxes and the trolley poles. At night cars were illuminated by rows of light bulbs.

With the population having reached the magical figure of 50,000 the question of an extension to Leagrave was again considered in 1911, at a joint meeting of the Leagrave and Limbury Parish Councils held on Friday 20 January, plans having been originally deposited the previous November. The route proposed by Balfour, Beatty was to continue from the Wardown terminus on to the Borough boundary, then turn sharp left and strike off across the fields on sleepered track on a private right of way to cross the lane to Biscot and Limbury, curving northwards on the line of Letchworth Road. Street track was to commence again in Limbury Road to Marsh Road where a right turn was to be made into that road, continuing to a terminus at a point 25 yards past the *Horseshoes* public house in the village of Leagrave. The total length of the Luton Light Railway (as it was to be known) was to be 1 mile 6 furlongs, of which approximately two thirds would be over private land. There were objections to this route on the grounds that it did not serve a sufficiently populated area between the town and Limbury and Leagrave. The Engineer for this scheme was a Mr H.L. Williams of London and the Parliamentary Agent was Mr John Kennedy of 25 Abingdon Street, Westminster, London.

Three other suggested routes were put forward, all of them stemming, not from the Wardown route, but from the Dunstable Road route. The longest of these was circular, originally proposed in March of 1908. This was to branch from the Dunstable Road line at the 'Trough' at Bury Park, along Leagrave Road, continue along Marsh Road to the *Horseshoes*, and turn into Grange Road (now Grange Avenue) to the *Sugar Loaf* pub. From here the line would return along Oak Road (now Oakley Road) turn left into Dunstable Road and rejoin the route at the Laundry terminus. A similar, but shorter, circular route was to commence at the Laundry and continue along Dunstable Road before turning into Beechwood Road. Almost at the end of this long road a right turn was to be made into Filmer Road, then along Gordon Road (now Memorial Road), parallel to the Midland Railway with an outlet onto Marsh Road, no particular point being specified, and then return to the 'Trough'. The route probably favoured by most residents, was a straightforward one from the 'Trough' along Leagrave Road and Marsh Road to as far as possible past the *Horseshoes* public house.

The promoters stuck to their original proposals stating that their route would give a journey time of five minutes from Leagrave to Wardown at fares of 1d per mile with the service operating to the Town Hall. They also affirmed that Workmen's Cars would be run. Strong objections were raised about the cost

of the extension because of a new system of so-called 'rail-less tramways' (trackless trolleys or trolley buses) which were coming on the scene. These, it was said, would cost only about £750 per mile as opposed to the proposed scheme which was said to be £4,950 per mile for a single line and £9,950 for double track. In spite of these objections the proposal by Balfour, Beatty was carried by both the Leagrave and Limbury Parish Council. Luton Council, incidentally, had been among the objectors, declaring that the trams on the Wardown route were likely to be overloaded (some hopes!) with 'foreigners' from Leagrave!

The Light Railway Commissioners sat on Monday 6 February 1911 at Luton Town Hall to receive the application for the Luton Light Railway put forward by Balfour, Beatty. In his submission, Mr Balfour said that the existing Corporation tramways did not pay and that the extension would help to improve that position, as a speed of 15 to 16mph could be attained on the Light Railway as opposed to the regulation Board of Trade speed of 10mph(?) on the existing street tramways. He also stated that the steepest gradient to be encountered would be 1 in 29. Fears were expressed regarding the weight of the tramcars on the poorly metalled roads of the parishes, but it was pointed out that traction engines of a greater weight than the 13-14 tons of a loaded tram were not banned from these same roads. Doubts were also raised as to whether the 18ft width of Limbury Road was sufficiently wide to permit of a single line of tramway. Mr Balfour assured everyone present that it was, and declared that in fact, if a road were

only 11ft wide it would be possible to lay a single track at one side instead of in the centre.

So as not to abstract traffic from the Midland Railway line from Leagrave into Luton, it was agreed to limit the use of the Light Railway to passengers and luggage not more than 28lb in weight and parcels not exceeding 250lb. The line would also be allowed to convey necessary materials for the construction and the electrical equipment, as well as for conveying water for the watering of the track.

By October the Light Railway Commissioners had agreed to Balfour, Beatty's application for the extension, subject to certain clauses. These were – that the Company should make good the breaking up of roads, construct the junction with the existing tramway, protect all drains and sewers, while the Corporation would grant running powers over the section from Wardown to the Town Hall. The proposed extension came to nothing for the Promoters withdrew, unable to agree to the conditions which the Light Railway Commissioners imposed upon them.

In spite of the fact that an extension to Leagrave was unsuccessful at least some sort of feeder service to and from Dunstable was in operation. By October 1910 The Dunstable Road Car Co., run by a colourful gentleman rejoicing in the improbable name of Hugh Snowie Beale Mackintosh Jones, of Downs Road, Dunstable, was operating (by agreement with Balfour, Beatty) a service with open top double deck buses to the Dunstable Road (Laundry) tram terminus, from the *Saracen's Head*, High Street South,

Car No.9 on Market Hill, heading for Park Square – taken from a commercial card, posted home to Aberdovey in Wales in July 1916.

Dunstable. It has been suggested that the vehicles were kept in the pub yard, but it is doubtful if they could have negotiated the entrance. On 12 December it was reported to the Luton Watch Committee that the buses were running right through to Luton town centre, in contravention of the agreement. Advertised as 'subject to continual alteration' by March 1911 only two journeys each way were being worked on Wednesdays and Saturdays with four each way on Sundays. For some part of the year one of the Sunday evening journeys connected with a bus from Leighton Buzzard.

The Bedfordshire Road Car Co. Ltd, of The Square, Dunstable, was formed to buy four second-hand Thornycroft buses from London General on 1 April 1911 and subsequently took over the bus services described in the previous paragraph. The new company was a joint venture of the aforementioned H.S.B.M. Jones and a Sydney Gerald Llewellyn Egremont, of Watling House, High Street, Dunstable. By the following October they were running five journeys each way on Sundays, but with dearer fares for the final trip of the day. However, at the close of the year only the Sunday workings remained and by April 1912 there was no service at all. Subsequently, in August, only one Sunday evening trip from Dunstable to Luton Town Hall was operated by Road Motors Ltd, becoming one each way by May 1913.

The Bedfordshire Road Car Co. Ltd was dissolved on 19 February 1915 and it was not until Service No.1 – Leighton Buzzard-Dunstable-Luton – of the National Omnibus and Transport Co. (predecessors of the Eastern National Omnibus Co.) started on 30 May 1920 that this important route was again covered.

Although the Luton tramways had been open less than three years, Councillor Impey asked the Tramways Committee in January of 1911 to give urgent attention to the state of the track on loops and sharp curves, particularly the loop at Cardiff Road and at the bottom of Ashton Road. The wear was so serious in some cases that only one side of the loop was being used. At the end of February the Borough Engineer reported that the straight track was in good order, but that there was some considerable wear on some of the sharp curves. It was not so bad as to require renewal, except in the case of the loop at Cardiff Road, which had been out of use for some time.

On the 27 July 1911 it was suggested by the Board of Trade to Luton Corporation that speed indicators should be fixed to the cars to enable motormen to better judge their speeds. The Tramways Committee resolved that Balfour, Beatty be approached and asked to fit one car with the necessary equipment in order to train drivers at estimating speeds. The outcome of this move is uncertain, but very few trams in any part of the country were equipped with speed indicators.

At a Town Council discussion on 5 September grave concern was expressed regarding overloading of the cars, when football matches were being played and also when fairs were run at Round Green. Councillor Oakley had seen cars pass his

house every evening with all the seats occupied and every inch of standing room, on top, inside, at the back of the car and even beside the driver, in use, contrary to the bye-laws. It was observed that the regulations regarding overloading were enforced in other towns so why shouldn't they be so in Luton? It was suggested that the police be asked to prosecute one or two of the offenders as an example to others. On football match days, the cars were probably loaded to twice their capacity. This was not so serious on the fairly level Dunstable Road route (where the Football Ground was situated) but overloading on the steep London Road and Round Green routes could be particularly dangerous.

Councillor Staddon ventured to express the opinion that maybe these complaints were being overlooked because the tramways were doing badly financially. The Mayor replied with an emphatic 'no': in fact the great thing that worried the Council was the *under*loading of the cars. Another member, Councillor Bone, considered that any injuries or fatalities sustained by passengers due to overcrowding would prove far more expensive to the Council than carrying a lesser load. The Town Clerk reported on 21 September that he had written to the Tramway Manager regarding the overloading problem but had not received a satisfactory reply. He was thereupon asked to write again. An application was reported from the Bedfordshire Road Car Co., to run two Leagrave buses; this, it was urged, should be allowed in order to bring the Tramways 'up to scratch'. It seems in the event that this was not permitted, a letter in the local paper declaring that the Tramways 'had to be bolstered up regardless of the needs of the people'.

At the beginning of October a lengthy petition bearing the names of many influential people in the High Town area complained to the Council about the noise of traffic over the granite setts between Midland Road and Havelock Road – that is, the double track kerbside section of tramway. The worthies requested that the setts be replaced by wood blocks similar to those outside the Chapel (High Town Methodist) 'as it was getting impossible to carry on normal business transactions and that both the Highways and Tramways Committees should do something about the nuisance'.

A letter from Balfour, Beatty was read at a Tramway Committee meeting on 26 October 1911, regarding a proposed extension of the tram depot by the addition of a storage room and a new paint shop. As it was said that the work would cost £200 'at the most', the committee was agreed on the desirability of the work. The balance of the Tramway Committee capital account stood at £252, so it was resolved that the extension be carried out.

Tram driving was not all that safe an occupation: witness the summoning by Mr E.J. Vaughan, the Tramway Manager, of a resident of Round Green for conduct 'likely to cause a breach of the peace' and assaulting Mr Ernest Shillingford, one of the drivers. As a result of his actions the accused was

fined 10/- and costs or seven days in gaol for using bad language and £2 and costs or 14 days for assaulting the driver.

Not only was driving a hazardous business; it seems that tram riding was too, as evidenced by the fact that a Mrs Adams claimed 10 guineas damages after being thrown off the platform of a car in Windsor Street due, allegedly to the tram jerking.

On 15 February 1912 a conductor was fined the sum of 50/- including costs for succumbing to temptation and stealing a book of tickets worth the princely sum of 1/- (i.e. twelve one penny tickets).

The advent of a National coal strike in the early part of 1912 was to curtail operations somewhat. The electricity works could not be operated at full power and some restriction had to be placed on the service. This did not affect the busy Dunstable Road route, but Round Green services were extended to every 40 minutes for part of the day instead of the usual 20 minute interval. On the Wardown route ordinary services ran until early afternoon and were then reduced to the frequency of the normal Sunday service for the rest of the day. Mr T.G. Hobbs in his locally famous 'Luton time Tables' published both the regular service times and also a 'strike supplement' in the April issue.

It appears that 1912 was a year fraught with incident. On 30 May under a heading in the local paper 'Luton Tramway system stopped' a taxi driver was accused of obstructing a tram during the previous week. It was alleged that Conway Road loop was blocked for a period of 18 minutes and as obstruction was a punishable offence under the Tramways Act 1870, the taxi driver was duly fined 40/- including costs. About this time, owing to deterioration of the tracks, trams frequently left the rails at the bottom of Ashton Road hill on the sharp bend opposite the *Hibbert Arms* public house. It was getting to be so frequent that people were beginning to wonder if it were wise to take a tram in wet weather. The main cause seemed to be the collection of silt in the grooved rails after it had been washed down the steep hill during severe rainstorms.

The journey time for the Dunstable Road route between Park Square and the Laundry varied between thirteen minutes and fifteen minutes. It required about two minutes only for a car entering service to reach Park Square from the Depot. From the Town Hall to Round Green the journey took approximately thirteen minutes, in spite of this being the shortest route, due no doubt to the adverse gradient all the way to the outer terminus. The run from London Road to Lansdowne Road on the Wardown route took fifteen minutes. It will thus be seen that the journey times on all three routes were fairly evenly balanced.

The regular weekday service on the Dunstable Road route commenced with an early car leaving Park Square at 5.43am and returning from the Laundry at 6.10am. This could well have been a special working for staff so that they could report for duty in ample time. The workmen's service proper began with a car every fifteen minutes for an hour, starting with the 7.15am from Park Square. At 8.20am the service was stepped

Car No.11 entering the long double track section in High Town Road; there is no cinema yet on the right, which places the view in the period before August 1912.

up to every ten minutes until 9.30am then reverting to a fifteen minute interval until noon. From midday onwards until 10 o'clock in the evening there was a car every ten minutes and for the final hour between 10 and 11 o'clock the service was at fifteen minute intervals. The last car outward on this route terminated at Conway Road, whence it returned at 11.11pm. The 9.50pm working from the town also stopped short at Conway Road. On Saturday evenings the cars continued every ten minutes for the last hour.

A feature of this route was the 'Workmen's Dinner Car'. This made two journeys from Bailey Street to Leagrave Road. The first was at 12.55pm from the depot, arriving at Leagrave Road at 1.08pm. A quick turn round must have ensued, as the timetable showed a departure at 1.08 also, giving an arrival back at Bailey Street at 1.17pm. The return working left at 1.44pm with an arrival at Leagrave Road the 'Trough' at 1.52pm. Where this car subsequently went is not clear from the timetable but it does not seem to have continued in revenue earning service.

In accordance with the decision of the Council in 1907 and in deference to the various religious bodies, Sunday tram services started at noon with a fifteen minute service. This continued throughout the afternoon until 5.00pm when the interval was decreased to ten minutes. The route shut down an hour earlier than during the week, with the last car running all the way to the Laundry, returning from there at 10.25 and matching the Depot at 10.40pm. Prior to 1914, timetables included short workings on the Round Green route, Bailey Street to

Jubilee Street, until curtailment to Mill Street and then subsequently to the Town Hall in the winter of 1910/11.

A peculiarity of the Round Green route was that the Mondays only services were the same as on Saturdays until 9.20pm, whereupon they reverted to a Tuesdays to Friday frequency. The service started at 8.16am from Bailey Street and continued at twenty minute intervals until 11.56am every weekday. For the rest of the day the service interval was reduced to twelve minutes, except for the mid-afternoon period on Tuesdays to Fridays when it remained at twenty minutes. The last car left Round Green at 11.10pm on weekdays and seven minutes later on Saturdays.

Sunday cars commenced with the 11.56am from Bailey Street and then ran every twenty minutes until teatime when the gap between them decreased to twelve minutes. Once again this route closed about an hour earlier than on weekdays, with the last car at 10.17pm from the outer terminus.

There are photographs showing 'High Town' on the destination blinds on this route. However it is not known for certain whether this was a regular short working. It may have been similar to the 'Workmen's Dinner Car' on the Dunstable Road route. If this was the case it is probable that the turn-back point was the curved loop at the bottom of High Town Road, at its junction with Midland Road. It is difficult to see the need for such a service. Owing to the circuitous nature of the route it was always a standing joke in the area that 'if you have time to spare you took the tram to High Town but if you were in a hurry you walked'. It may be that,

due to staff shortages during the Great War, some services were curtailed at this point – in the photograph referred to, for instance, there is a wartime conductress.

The Wardown route was probably the most straightforward as regards its service. It started from Lansdowne Road in the winter at 8.15am and operated on a thirty minute headway until noon each weekday. The frequency was then increased to fifteen minutes until 8.45 in the evenings. After that time the interval was half-hourly until 10.30pm on Mondays to Fridays. On Saturdays the cars continued every quarter of an hour until 10.45pm. On Sundays the trams started at noon and ran every thirty minutes until the last car terminated at the Cheapside loop in George Street at 10.15, whence it continued to the Depot.

The Council had the option of determining the lease without payment of compensation after five or fifteen years and as the first five years expired in February 1913, the question was debated at a meeting on 22 October 1912. At this time the voting was 16 to 8 in favour of giving Balfour, Beatty & Co. notice to continue with the lease for a second period, this time of ten years. The annual instalments of principal and interest upon the £63,000 capital were to be payable by the lessees.

After holding the post of General Manager since October 1911, Mr E.J. Vaughan was appointed Engineer and Manager in July 1913, at which time Mr J.W. Maskell became General Manager for a short period. He was succeeded by Mr H.G. Merrick in August 1914.

CHAPTER 4

THE WAR YEARS (1914-1918)

Runaway Tramcar
Working Arrangements
Condition of Tramways

Car No.2 on the Town Hall loop in July 1915, in a sea of people. The occasion is a civic reception for the 1st/5th. Beds Territorials (The Yellow Devils) before their departure for Gallipoli. Note the proliferation of straw hats and the famous Luton Boater; also three straw hatted policemen near the front of the tram and the Bundy time clock on the pole.

Even at the start of the Great War, Luton still retained the character and air of a small country town, with open fields stretching out beyond the end of the tram tracks. In fact between the terminus at the Laundry in Dunstable Road and Church Street railway bridge in Dunstable stood only one house, in a quiet country road. This was known as the Halfway House and stood near the junction of the present-day M1 motorway. The tram terminus in Round Green was at the limit of the 'built-up' area from the town direction and was surrounded on the remaining sides by open fields.

It has been estimated that during the First World War as many as 25,000 soldiers were billeted in private houses, church halls and vacant premises, apart from the large army camps which were established at both Biscot Mill and Luton Hoo. The town, which now boasted a population of about 57,000, was crowded with soldiers throughout the whole of the war and there is no doubt that some of the tram services were disrupted on occasions such as when, on 5 June 1915, the 1st/5th Beds. Territorials, known as the 'Yellow Devils' marched from Bedford to attend a civic reception at the Town Hall in their honour, before embarkation to Gallipoli. Wardown House, in Wardown Park and previously run by the civic authorities as a restaurant, was transformed into a Military hospital and the trams on the Wardown

services would probably have been at their busiest conveying visitors to this establishment. In spite of their needs services were curtailed as a wartime economy to the Lansdowne Road loop. This measure lasted for the whole of the period August 1914 to November 1918. As more men went off to the War, men were replaced by women conductresses.

Incidents involving troops occurred from time to time – sometimes of a quite hair-raising nature. In September 1914 shots were fired at the tram driven by Motorman Mr E. Price when it stopped at the top of High Town Road. About fifty soldiers were on board but none sustained injury. An exhaustive search was mounted lasting about two hours, which proved unsuccessful. On another occasion a two-horse army waggon was in collision with a tram driven by Motorman Clark. It is to be supposed that it came off worse in the encounter. However these were only minor occurrences in a country so deeply engaged in military conflict.

Mr A.E. Wray came to Luton in 1915 as Manager. He had previously been Assistant Manager (from January 1912) of the South Metropolitan Electric Tramways & Lighting Co. Ltd, in the Croydon and Mitcham area. He was subsequently made Superintendent, from 14 June 1913 when control of the 'Southmet' passed to the

London & Suburban Traction Co. This itself was a tramway holding company, established on 20 November 1912 jointly by the British Electric Traction and the Underground Electric Railways Co. of London Ltd (the Underground Group).

Notwithstanding some steep hills and five curves of between 36 feet and 49 feet radius, accidents were fortunately few. One serious one did occur however, just after the Christmas holiday at about 11.20am on 28 December 1916. Car No.8 was running towards the town centre from the direction of Round Green down the fairly steep section of Midland Road, when it failed to negotiate the sharp left-hand bend into Old Bedford Road. It left the rails, charged the Midland Railway embankment, rammed a tramway standard and damaged a low wall. Seven people were injured, including a young boy and girl from the same family and the Acting Chief Constable of Luton, Mr Hagley.

The driver, Mr Lloyd, was trapped and found unconscious at the controls with one hand on the emergency electric brake 'which was switched right over'. Rescue work was immediately started by some soldiers from a local unit and they were further assisted by police organised by Mr Hagley in spite of the pain of a dislocated shoulder. A crowbar had to be used to lift some of the wreckage to free the driver. The front platform was severely damaged and the floor of the saloon torn up. Some of the seats were ripped from their mountings and the staircase crushed and forced back towards the bulkhead. Passengers were injured by flying glass from broken windows and numerous splinters of wood. The car was eventually moved by noon, under the direction of the Manager and Inspectors Duncombe and Janes. The conductor, Mr Eaton, sustained a severely cut lip, bruises and shock.

When interviewed by the press Mr Wray, the Tramways Manager (he had previously held a similar post with the Gravesend & Northfleet Tramways, from April 1914 to 1915) could give no immediate explanation for the crash. He said the car was equipped with four types of brakes, two mechanical and two electrical and that the cause would remain a mystery only the driver could answer. Mr Lloyd, who was 46, was locally trained and had twelve months' experience. The car had made seven previous journeys to Round Green that morning without trouble and had been overhauled only three months previously. When reunited with the track No.8 was mechanically still in working order. The tramways had been running for nearly nine years, and carried about 16,000,000 fare-paying passengers and this was the first time any passenger had been badly injured. The car was severely damaged and it was many months before it appeared again in service. The Town Clerk wrote to the Board of Trade to enquire if it would be necessary to hold a public enquiry but this, it turned out, was not likely as there was no fatality. Until a few years ago it was still possible to distinguish, by the different colour of the replacement bricks, where the tram hit the wall.

Services during the War years proved to be somewhat erratic. Around April 1914 the Dunstable Road service was extended at the southern end from Park Square to Bailey Street (the Depot) replacing the Round Green service which then terminated at the Town Hall. At the same time the Wardown trams were curtailed to the Lansdowne Road loop. Pre-war the Winter service terminated at this point, being extended to Wardown (West Lodge) on Monday to Friday evenings and on Saturdays and Sundays during the summer.

Possibly in an attempt to maximise on the number of available serviceable cars – many were under long-term repair, due no doubt to lack of staff and spares – the London Road to Wardown service varied almost daily. At the latter end of the War there was a basic frequency of 36 minutes advertised by Hobbs in his timetable, with a note to the effect that if two cars were available for this route 'a notice would be displayed at the Town Hall'. This was not much consolation for passengers waiting at Lansdowne Road. However, as this terminal point was less than three quarters of a mile from the Town Hall, many residents eschewed the trams and did not mind walking into town, as indeed they do today along the pleasant and level New Bedford Road alongside the park.

There were reports of the whole system coming to a halt for several hours at a time in the later War years. A couple of simultaneous breakdowns or derailments at strategic points could easily have brought about total disruption. Perhaps as a result of the poor performance there was a proposal put forward in 1917 for the introduction of trolleybuses, along with the complete replacement of the tramway system. This

would probably have overcome the problems of obstruction caused by the hat manufacturers' carts and drays at kerbside locations in the town centre. Yet most such vehicles were of German manufacture (Cedes-Stoll) and obviously supplies had ceased by that time. The proposal was shelved, somewhat naturally, until peacetime conditions returned. The possibility of trolleybuses in Luton was resurrected in 1929 when some consideration was given to extensions in the Lea Ward, but nothing came of the proposals.

Two tram drivers had lucky escapes when their cars collided about 7.30am on the morning of 19 February 1917, on the single line near Waldeck Road on the Dunstable Road route. Motorman C. Simpkins was driving the first car into town, with five or six passengers on board from the Laundry terminus, when it appeared he decided to pass the outgoing car at the Gas Works loop instead of the more usual place, Beech Road. The other car, with motorman Hinds in charge and carrying 18 passengers, had already left the Gas Works loop and a collision in the thick fog was inevitable. It is surprising there were no injuries as Simpkins' car had the platform buckled and the front smashed in. The other car only suffered slight damage and was off the road for a day or two. Owing to the amount of damage to the front end of Simpkins' car it could not be towed. It was pushed back to the Beech Road loop where Hinds' car passed and it was subsequently pushed all the way to the Depot, causing an hour's delay to the service. The badly damaged tram was out of action for some months. It is an interesting fact that this made it the fifth car to be 'hors de combat' at that particular time.

The worst tramway accident in Luton, 28th December 1916. Car No.8 jumped the rails at the bottom of Midland Road hill, ramming a traction pole and a low brick wall. Seven people were injured including a young boy and girl and the acting Chief Constable, Mr Hagley. No.8 did not get back into service for eighteen months.

Top. The 'hub' of the Luton system. This is a commercial postcard, posted during the Great War, in November 1916 by a soldier Bert to his Dad in North London. His camp was by the Midland main line about twenty minutes from Luton station ' a decent place, plenty of fresh air'.

Middle. The Town Hall, with Car No.3 en route to Wardown. The card was posted on 19th May 1919; it was hot 'we are roasted and dead beat', Win wrote to her niece in Yorkshire.

Bottom. Luton is hardly notable in the long roll call of civil unrest in Britain but when the Council refused permission for various ex-servicemen's organisations to use Wardown Park for a Thanksgiving Service and Peace Celebration, the reaction was a far from peaceful one. On the evening of 19th July 1919 a crowd invaded the Town Hall and set light to the ground floor, using petrol conveniently stolen from Franklin's Temperance Commercial Hotel pumps nearby. The present building was not finally completed until 1936.

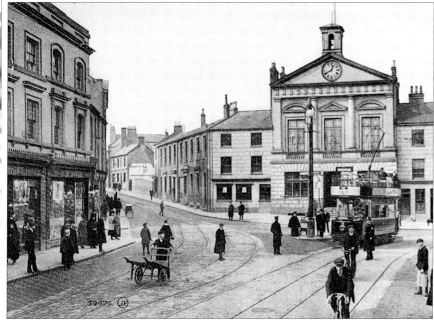

Obviously, nearly half the rolling stock out of action amounted to a very serious situation. With only seven cars available it would have been difficult to maintain the advertised service.

Apparently the serious accident in Midland Road had very little effect on the other drivers as five of them were in court in mid-July 1917 accused of reckless driving. They were mostly middle-aged men but one 17-year old discharged soldier was said to have allowed a 15-year old boy conductor to drive on another occasion alongside Wardown Park. He was also stated to have often had women conductors on the driving platform with him, contrary to the regulations. One of the older men had been driving for two months and had not seen the official regulations regarding speed limits. Mr Wray agreed to examine the men in his office on the regulations in the future. All the accused were found guilty and were fined sums varying between 5/- and 20/-.

One outcome of the Midland Road smash was a court case which was heard in mid-August 1917. A female straw hat machinist sued the tramway company for loss of wages. In evidence it was stated that she earned an average of 30/- per week and hadn't been able to do this since the accident. She claimed loss of wages amounting to £39.10.0 and in addition 10/6d which she had to pay for a medical certificate. The tramway company admitted negligence and she was awarded £60 damages.

In early 1918, in order to conserve energy, the President of the Board of Trade notified all tramway undertakings that they must reduce coal consumption by 15%. Later, in June of the same year he requested that the number of stops on tramways be reduced.

At the end of July and the beginning of August 1918, the tramway men staged two strikes, both on a Sunday, one of which was at the Bank Holiday. They only lasted until mid-morning and very few people realised they had even taken place! The men claimed

Two trams in George Street, by the Town Hall, before the First World War.

a rate of 6d per hour, but eventually settled for 5d instead of the 4½d they had been getting. In addition, the bonus for men was increased to £1 per week and 10/- for the girls. Mr Wray pointed out that the company was already complying with the Award of the Government Committee and in fact paying considerably more than that award. If a driver worked a full six day week he couldn't earn less than £2.15.0 and a conductor not less than £1.15.0.

Owing to greatly increased expenses because of war conditions, pay awards, and so on, the fares were increased from 19

August 1918, probably under the provisions of a piece of legislation passed earlier in the year known as the 'Statutory Undertakings (Temporary Increase of Charges) Act'. Naturally there were protests about this, but when the Town Council investigated they found them reasonable and not more than the equivalent of 1d per mile.

The condition of the tramways came under attack from the Council in October and December 1918. The Manager countered that the cars were quite safe and in a good condition under the present circumstances and that, 'the labour position and weather

permitting' the track would soon be repaired. He also revealed that the Board of Trade did not consider a public enquiry necessary for the Midland Road smash, as the car was found to be in good mechanical condition.

In their yearly report at the beginning of 1919, Balfour, Beatty admitted to the Council that the tramways were not all they should be, but this was entirely due to both the labour and material shortages owing to the war. The track was in reasonably good condition except in three or four places in Dunstable Road and the overhead installation was in good condition, in their opinion. They

Car No.2 with its proud crew, alongside the 'Moor' and bound for London Road, in the first year or so of the tram's operation.

In a scene hardly imaginable today, casting an eye round modern Luton, a Car bound for Park Street makes its way along Manchester Street.

proposed to put up a system of signal lighting which would eliminate a lot of the dissatisfaction with the service. This was presumably for signalling the passing loops so that a more intensive service could be run. No more was heard of this proposal however!

Six of the cars had been electrically overhauled and repainted, and others were being done at that time, and in a few months all would be in a good condition. The frames of some of the cars had begun to sag by this time and no doubt part of the overhaul consisted of bracing the bodies at the corners, as is evident in some of the photographs.

Like many others the company had encouraged their employees to enlist in the armed forces, but as a consequence had to contend with poor quality labour. There was also a considerable turnover in labour and since the beginning of the war no less than *two hundred* men had been trained as drivers by the Manager, in spite of the fact that the company could only employ about fifteen at any one time. As soon as a man had been trained to drive, he left to go into one of the many munitions factories, where he could get higher wages as an unskilled man. However, it was encouraging that the number of car-miles worked had increased during the past four years. Most of these were no doubt due to the increased number of troops and munitions workers in the area.

At this time Alderman Wilkinson took the opportunity of expressing the Tramway Committee's appreciation of Mr Wray, who was resigning and leaving the town. He had to work under difficult wartime conditions but was a most excellent Manager

and had taken a lively interest in the undertaking.

All tramway undertakings signed an agreement in March 1919 with the Municipal Tramways Conference, Tramways and Light Railways Association and the National Transport Workers Federation, for a working week of 48 hours, with no working day longer than eight hours. Four National Bank holidays would be granted – Easter Monday, Whit Monday, August Bank Holiday and Boxing Day, and if workers were obliged to work on those days they would be paid at 1¼ times the rate, as was the first two hours of any weekday overtime beyond the basic eight hour working day. Subsequent overtime was to be paid at 1½ times the rate.

Towards the end of 1919 there was some development along New Bedford Road and following protests the usual winter curtailment of the Wardown route was cancelled – though the service frequency was increased to every 40 minutes.

In 1919 a tramway employee wishing to become a tramdriver spent most of his time in the Depot doing odd jobs, such as cleaning the accumulated dirt from the wheels, brake blocks and armatures of the cars. He also cleaned the inside of the car and collected the discarded tickets – general husbandry in fact, so that he became thoroughly acquainted with the cars and their working. Unlike many large systems Balfour, Beatty had no official driver training scheme and in order to learn to drive he first had to obtain permission, and then, in his spare time persuade a colleague to show him the ropes. This amounted to an odd hour in the evenings. At

this rate four to six weeks were required to become proficient. In between times he would go out on the cars as a spare conductor covering for sick colleagues, rest day working and holiday relief.

From his fellow qualified motormen he would learn to 'notch up' when starting off with the motors connected in series, to half speed for the first five notches on the controller thereby progressively cutting out the resistances. The final four notches cut out further resistances with the motors in parallel, until maximum speed was achieved. Most motormen used the track brake on the steep hills of Ashton Road, Beech Hill and Hightown Road/Midland Road. The single deck one-man operated car introduced in 1923 was slightly different to the twelve double-deckers as its Westinghouse controller had only seven notches and was equipped with rheostatic braking. This car was restricted to certain experienced motormen only and would not be used to train novices.

In the 1920s the working day was split into two shifts, commonly known as early turn and late turn. The early turn started at 6.30am with the first car on the Dunstable Road route and the late turn finished with the last car on this same route at 11.30pm or thereabouts. Motormen usually worked a four week period on the Dunstable Road, two weeks on Round Green and two weeks on Wardown routes. Less than twenty motormen were employed and as the usual number of cars in use at ordinary times was eight, this meant there were probably only seventeen in all – that is, eight multiplied by two shifts plus one spare. Any additional peak hour cars were probably driven by 'passed conductors' – men whose usual job was conducting but who were also competent in tram driving. The spare crew were on stand-by to cover any emergencies which might occur and spent most of their time on the track cleaning out the points which continually became clogged with dirt and debris. When the eight minute service was in operation on the Dunstable Road route the passing places were the Gas Works loop and Conway Road loop. The operation of points was carried out by the motorman using a point iron, to move the point blades over. On the occasion of fêtes or fairs in Wardown Park extra cars, colloquially known as 'swingers' were run from the Town Hall for the convenience of the public.

It has been said by certain motormen that when the 'Stattie' (Statute) fair was held at the Corn Exchange in the early days the cars did not run past that point to Park Square but terminated at the Town Hall. However, this must be open to some doubt, as others interviewed maintain that this was not so.

As there were no public houses in the Dunstable Road area beyond *The Fox* by Dallow Road and Luton was not a particularly abstemious place, the cars on that route were usually fairly busy bringing people into the town in the evenings. Evening traffic on the Round Green route was different in character however, as there were plenty of hostelries in High Town. In fact Round Green was known by the motormen as the 'wet-end' of town, in view of the three pubs situated at the terminus.

Probably the most serious disruption of the tram services which occurred after the 1914-1918 War was on 19 July 1919. The Council had refused permission for various ex-servicemen's organisations to use Wardown Park for a Thanksgiving Service and Peace Celebration. The Council's own plans were consequently disrupted and during the evening the disgruntled crowds ransacked the Town Hall and started a fire on the ground floor which was fed with petrol taken from the pumps outside the nearby Franklins Temperance Commercial Hotel. The Riot Act was subsequently read to the crowds. The Town Hall was gutted and it was not until 1936 that the present building was finally completed. One consequence was that certain of the Tramways Committee's records were seriously damaged and stained by water.

On 23 September 1919 responsibility for all tramway matters nationally passed from the Board of Trade to the Ministry of Transport.

Apparently, little action was taken as a result of the Council's notice to the Company of 17 December 1918, to put the tramways into a reasonable state of repair by 30 June 1919. Things had come to a pretty pass and therefore on 16 December 1919 it was resolved that the lessees be furnished with a list of specific complaints from a four page report of Mr J.W. Tomlinson AMICE, the Borough Engineer and Surveyor. The list reveals a sorry state of affairs. There were loose rail joints, displaced setts, overwide grooves and consequently narrow treads and corrugations in the track. There were loose and worn points, some with pieces of wood in place of the moveable tongue and blocked drains. Both at the London Road and Wardown terminus the loops were not used and cars did not go to the end of the tracks. The story of the overhead was no better. Old guard and span wires were hanging from poles all over the system and pull-off wires were out of order and had been so for a very considerable time. In fact no voltage drop readings had been taken for many years despite this being a Board of Trade requirement. In fact it would have been a very serious matter if they had a claim for damage to gas or water mains as a result of electrolysis. Poles also had finials missing and needed painting to overcome corrosion. Feeder boxes were out of order and in fact one was smashed and had been removed. As regards the cars, those that had not been previously overhauled had loose seats, broken lifeguards, ventilating windows screwed up and noisy gearing.

The Company was requested to execute the improvement works to the cars and overhead by 31 March 1920 and to the track by 31 May 1920. In the meantime they were to promptly remedy the more serious defects especially those in the track, which were considered unsafe. If the works were not completed to the Council's satisfaction they would undertake them and charge the cost to the Company.

Further discussion ensued and it came to light that the report practically amounted to the condoning of the arrears of ten years of neglected maintenance. It now seemed the Council were the doubtful possessors of an undertaking which would cost four to five times the amount it would have done if repairs had been carried out as the need arose. Because of all this – the poor track, sagging overhead, cars under repair and all the rest of it – the advertised service between 1920-22 was much reduced compared to 1919 and was withdrawn on Sundays during the winters.

Park Street, in a Great War era postcard.

CHAPTER 5

THE CORPORATION TAKES OVER

The General Strike
Abandonment Talk
Closure and Scrapping

Sagging with old age, some time after 1923 Car No.10 is about to leave from the 'wrong' side of the Town Hall loop, bound for Round Green. Note the policeman's straw helmet.

After the lessees had operated the tramways for almost fifteen years without profit, until the last year of the lease and with varying degrees of success (Sunday services were withdrawn altogether by February of 1921) the Council stepped in and exercised its option and took over the running of all the routes from 21 February 1923. Things improved somewhat, Sunday services were restored and week-day frequencies were considerably improved. From that date Mr W.W. Clarke (who had been Balfour, Beatty's acting local manager for the past four years) was duly appointed Manager by the Corporation. His experience was gained during three years in the Electrical and Civil Engineers Department of Glasgow Corporation tramways, where his father Mr William Clarke had been the first Chief Engineer. Subsequently he spent three years with the Caledonian Railway before returning for a further two years as a draughtsman on power and substation extensions and the design of rolling stock for Glasgow. From there he ventured to Lisbon where he stayed six years in the capacity of Assistant Engineer to the Companhia Carris de Ferro de Lisboa, a local company, wholly-owned by the British Lisbon Electric Tramways Ltd. This was

followed by his appointment as Manager of the Inverness tramway system for 3½ years and then a further year as Works Manager of a steam and electric crane manufacturer by the name of J. Henderson & Co. before coming to Luton.

There was agitation amongst Luton's 58,000 population in February for a return to the 1d fares of the War years but the Tramway Committee could not recommend this due to a reduction in receipts. The year ending 31 January 1919 proved to be the year during which the greatest number of passengers had been carried, while during 1922 the total passengers had amounted to 2,150,694, a return of 1Nd per passenger. Discussions took place with a view to making economies and the Council were of the opinion that £600 per annum could be saved on administrative costs.

By 23 March, the Corporation's operation of the system was not proving all that successful, as witnessed by the fact that the electricity consumption had increased by 42% compared with February 1922. Frequent breakdown also occurred in the feeder cable from the Electricity Works, under Church Street, which was found to be defective due to the penetration of water. £500, it was said, would be required for the laying of a new

cable from the Power Station, along St Mary's Road and Church Street to Park Square.

It was decreed by the Tramways Committee on 3 May 1923 that the tram shelter at the Laundry terminus in Dunstable Road should be locked every night before the last tram left for the Depot.

About this same time the Manager was instructed to report on the feasibility of discontinuing the through London Road – Wardown route and substituting a Wardown – Park Street service and also a Chapel Street - London Road service. He was then instructed to investigate the possibility of a 'one-man' car on this lightly used cross-town route, with a view to economical use of both manpower and traction current. The second course of action was chosen and subsequently the one and only addition to the fleet was an ex-horse car from Glasgow Corporation, acquired on 21 May 1923. It was originally No.118 in their fleet and a double-decker, though it was cut down to single deck at Luton. The idea was an economy measure and it was operated on the lightly trafficked Wardown route as a 'one-man' front exit car.

The method of working the 'one-man' car was for all the passengers to take their seats after boarding, when the

Back in earlier days, before the Corporation took over (probably before the Great War in fact) Car No.1 with accompanying posed group (staff perhaps?) stands on Villa Road loop, alongside the 'Moor'.

motorman (often one Stan Perkins) would go around and collect all the fares before moving off from the stop. For these extra duties and responsibilities he was paid an additional farthing per hour.

Before the introduction of this car, the route had been worked by two double-deck cars but henceforth, until closure, it was worked by one double-decker and the ex-Glasgow car. Luton, unlike Exeter, Peterborough and Plymouth, was not superstitious and allocated the fleet number 13 to this car; however, it was known locally as the 'new tram', notwithstanding the fact that it was the oldest in the fleet, a fact probably unknown to the general public.

It is uncertain what profits were made up to this period but a report dated 20 May 1926 in the *Luton News* quoted the following figures:-

Year	1924/5	1925/6
Income	£18,041	£18,635
Gross Profit	£12,511	£12,204
Net Profit	£ 1,168	£ 1,876

The number of passengers carried in an average year at this period totalled 2,316,976.

'Nobby' Clarke, the General Manager who came from Glasgow, was a stickler for discipline, as was Councillor Albert Wilkinson, Chairman of the Tramways Committee, who lived at 'The Chase' in Hitchin Road. He would walk to Round Green to catch the tram into town and if he caught one of the employees in any of the three pubs there they would be in trouble.

In fact conductors were admonished for disposing of their excess change to the publicans and one employee received a 'telling-off' for using the lavatory facilities behind the *Shepherd and Flock* pub.

With such a small workforce most of the drivers were well known to the prominent members of the community who occasionally used to tip them for stopping the car and setting them down outside their front doors. However, woe betide any driver who failed to wait for a Town Councillor or businessman or left a stop a few minutes ahead of the appointed time.

No specific arrangements were made for the crews to take meal breaks. Hasty snacks were the order of the day at the terminus, or sandwiches would be eaten on the move, at the controls. Some of the more generous residents would occasionally supply the crews with hot meals and the ubiquitous 'billy' can of tea was always in evidence.

With regard to uniforms; probably until the time Luton Corporation took over, the drivers wore serge jackets with leather cuffs. They had ten buttons, and stand-up collars and were kept buttoned up to the neck. A flat topped peak cap was worn with a metal badge inscribed 'Motorman'. In later years the jacket had a lay-flat collar and broad lapels which could be buttoned close to the neck. The conductor's uniform was similar, with the addition of the Bell Punch machine which was worn on the left side and the leather money bag on the right. More than likely the whistle would be fastened to one of the straps. A better quality jacket was worn by

Inspectors, with concealed buttons and a high collar inscribed 'Inspector' on each side of the fastening. This was repeated on the front of their peaked caps, which also had a gold band.

High buttoned greatcoats were also worn in colder weather by conductors, motormen and Inspectors alike. To combat bad weather motormen were also issued with a mackintosh or cape, a Sou'wester and Wellington boots. In really cold weather, tales have it, it was not unusual for a driver to arrive home after his turn of duty with his mackintosh frozen stiff and stand it up indoors for it to thaw... Conductresses employed during the Great War sported hip length jackets with flat collars, epaulettes, lapels and patch pockets worn with a wide skirt which reached almost to the ankles. The uniform was finished off with buttoned boots, a wide-brimmed hat and the Bell Punch and money bag.

In April 1926 Mr Roland Henry Nuttall was appointed Engineer and Manager, the post he was to retain until the closure of the tramways. He had previously been with Doncaster Corporation Tramways, on the engineering side of that undertaking.

One motorman recalled a bad thunderstorm which occurred in the 1920s, lasting for two days. Heavy rain flooded the town centre and rats were seen running about, having been driven out of the blocked drains. As he was negotiating the Cheapside loop, the car was struck by lightning. A pyrotechnic display followed which eventually melted the meter, burnt out the resistances under the stairs and also melted the brass hand stanchion on the platform. More flashes ensued when an attempt was made to re-wire the trolley onto the overhead.

Minor electric shocks were often experienced by the crews, in spite of the trolleys being earthed and fitted with a trolley standard leakage indicator. These incidents, along with the lack of protection from bad weather were accepted as hazards of the job.

When the General Strike of May 1926 reared its ugly head, the tramway employees were not unanimous as to whether they should join their colleagues in similar capacities or not, and some services continued running. During and after the strike, when there was a shortage of coal and consequently electrical power, the Chairman of the Tramways Committee was criticised for wasting electricity by maintaining the tramway services. He is reported as saying that in fact the tramways consumed only as little as 2% of the total available output of the electricity power station during the period of the shortage. After the settlement of the strike twenty motormen and conductors who had left work acknowledged their error in a joint letter to the Tramways Committee, asking that they should not be penalised by loss of their holiday entitlement.

By this time Luton's population had grown to a round figure of 62,000 and the town made preparations for the occasion of the Jubilee of the Borough, on 30th June. As part of the celebrations connected with this event, decorated floats and flat waggons were pulled over the tracks by horses.

Photographs indicate that stop signs reading ALL CARS STOP HERE were mounted approximately 10-12 feet high; that is, about halfway up, on the tramway standards. Why such an elevated position was chosen is difficult to say, but presumably it would have made them plainly visible from a distance.

Councillor Chapman, speaking of the fact that there was no car service in Park Street said *'At present a tram is like a bad boy – it goes out early in the morning, stays out all day and only returns home to bed'*. This was a reference to the fact that the Dunstable Road service at that time was operated mainly from Park Square and not the Depot. After a period of inactivity, one month's trial was approved, on 23 June 1927, for the carriage of passengers between Park Square and the Depot. 1928 saw the incorporation of the village of Leagrave within the Borough of Luton, but it was no nearer to obtaining a tramway extension than when the subject was first broached in 1911.

In the annual report of January 1929 some consideration was given to the provision of public transport to Lee Ward.

With the question of an extension to the tramway in mind, some thought must have been given to a route under the Church Street/ Hitchin Road railway bridges, as the use of single-deck tramcars was mentioned. The use of trolley buses or motor buses was also considered but nothing seems to have come of these suggestions.

In common with many other similar small systems, Luton's was not progressively modernised and it was not until the first rumblings of closure talk in mid-1929 that four Brush top covers were purchased, for the sum of £1,155. They were fitted to cars 1, 2, 4 and 5, the first car so treated being given a trial run on the Saturday preceding 11 June. Their appearance was enhanced and these handsome vehicles were thereafter used almost exclusively on the more prestigious Dunstable Road route. The many workers who used it must have been suitably appreciative of the enclosed top deck. No doubt many wondered why only four cars were so treated, especially as this service used at least six cars during the peak periods.

Although the trams made almost £2,000 profit in 1925-26, by the beginning of 1929 it had dropped to half that figure. In spite of this, in reply to various complaints about the efficiency of the service the *Luton News* leader on 3 January asked *'Why scrap the trams when they make a profit of £1,000 a year?'*. It pointed out that this course would mean an immediate cost to the ratepayers (in difficult times) of £20,000 for loan repayments, which otherwise would be spread over about thirty years. A correspondent of the paper was not so enthusiastic about the trams. He stated *'The chief argument for the survival of the trams is that buses could not cope with the rush hour loads – that three buses would be required for every tram. Perhaps it is forgotten that removal of the trams would leave the whole width of the road available for free-moving vehicles'*. Such sentiments have a familiar ring today, with regard to buses in traffic jam packed city streets. It is no doubt very true that the great increase of motor traffic since the Great War did affect the speed of the trams, as well as the single track with passing loop installation. It would have been very difficult however to have doubled the track, particularly in the town centre (where it would have been most beneficial) owing to the narrowness of the streets, many of which have lasted to the present day

After almost twenty years of service, deterioration of the system was very evident and track maintenance, which had cost £1,517 in 1927, rose to £2,792 in 1930. Some consideration was also given to renewal of the overhead trolley wire, but by that time it was found that the cost of replacing and restringing the overhead was £80 per mile – about £1,000 for the whole system. Needless to say, given subsequent events, this work was not carried out.

Talk of abandoning the trams came to a head when, near the end of 1930 the Eastern National Omnibus Co. Ltd (subsequently United Counties) made an offer of £64,000 in cash for the purchase of the Luton Tramways. Part of the deal was

'Redrup & Starkings Ltd – Service, Satisfaction'! **Car No.5 on the Dunstable Road route descending Upper George Street, in 1931. Note the arms carrying the wires, bracketed off the buildings, and the warning sign with triangle in middle distance. Christ Church can be faintly discerned in the background.**

A postcard view, showing what is probably Car No.9 after 1923, on the 'wrong' side of the Town Hall Loop and waiting departure to Round Green.

that the Corporation would retain the freehold properties and other tangible assets, and that the Company would engage Mr Roland Henry Nutthall, then Tramway Engineer and Manager, in a suitable position at a salary of not less than £500 per annum. The Company also agreed to take over as many of the other tramway employees as might be suitable. The Corporation, on its part, was to covenant not to engage in any form of passenger transport for the next 21 years. Up to this time the tramways had cost the initial £63,000 plus a capital outlay of £65,928 since the inauguration of the system. Previous to the Company's offer the Council had recommended the substitution of the tramcars by trolleybuses and five motor buses at a total cost of £56,000. Moreover, road costs of £2,285 were to be made a charge on the rates.

The proposal to sell the trams along with the transport rights caused the biggest controversy of the inter-war years in the town. Factions became sharply divided, those more socialistically minded being reluctant to relinquish the transport rights and the remainder keen to accept the cash offer of the bus company. Even the two local newspapers (owned by the same firm) took sides at the height of the argument with the *Luton News* all in favour of selling and the *Saturday Telegraph* resolutely opposed to any sale. When the Corporation finally agreed to sell, the *Saturday Telegraph's* placards most effectively merely proclaimed the one word 'SOLD'. At a meeting of the Council on 20 January 1931 the Company's offer was accepted by 17 votes to 7.

The fight was not over however, the 'Luton Ratepayers Association' strongly protesting in a resolution passed by its members; it asked the Minister of Transport to intervene. The Minister ruled, on 12 May 1931, that under the terms of Section 44 of the Tramways Act 1870, the Corporation could not enter into an agreement which did not contemplate the disposal of the freehold property, track, overhead equipment or rolling stock as well as the goodwill. Section 44 of the Act concerned deals with 'Powers of Sale' and states briefly that *'Where any tramway ... has been opened for ... six months the promoters may with the consent of the Board of Trade* (by then Ministry of Transport) *sell to any ... company ... and when any such sale has been made all the rights powers authorities obligations and liabilities ... shall be transferred to, and vested in ... the company to whom the same has been sold ...'* The Eastern National, however, did not want the fixed and moving assets of the tramway and the bargain, which appeared so eminently satisfactory from the Council's point of view, was consequently squashed by the highest authority. This is the reason the Corporation ran the familiar red buses alongside the green Company ones of the United Counties (ex-Eastern National) until 3 January 1970 when history was repeated by the successors to the Eastern National taking over the successors to the trams. Nothing is very static in the public transport business, however – no pun intended. With the de-regulation of the industry by the Minister of Transport, Nicholas Ridley MP from 1 January 1986,

United Counties was split into three units. The Luton & District portion reverted to a livery of red and ivory reminiscent of the old Luton Corporation bus colours. The trams were not saved, however, by the Minister's earlier decision of 1931 and the Corporation decided in favour of motor buses, which it planned to run over and beyond the old tram routes. For this purpose some of the tram drivers were trained to drive the new buses.

It was only with the impending closure of the tramways that the population of the town reached the figure of 70,000, a figure, ironically, which one of the early promoters in 1903 had declared to be suitable for a viable tramway system.

Commenting on the Minister's decision, the then President of the Luton Chamber of Commerce, stated: *'considering that the trams are an out of date method of transport, the sale of the system would appear to be an advantage to the town. One does not hear nowadays of any municipality proposing to institute trams and that, surely, is proof that this method of transport no longer is desirable or fulfils the purpose it once did'.* At the same time Mr Thomas Keens, a former member of the House of Commons, and chairman of the British Section of the Road and Rail Co-ordination Committee at the recent Washington Congress, was asked by the press about the proposals for tramways in England. He replied *'... that there was no future for tramways in England, and were it not for the difficulties attendant on local Government finance, the existing trams would have been scrapped long ago in most provincial centres'* ...and this was in 1931. In point of fact there was a wholesale closing down of tramways in the late 1920s and early 1930s. Forty-seven municipal and sixteen company tramways closed in the second half of that decade.

In the first instance it was agreed by the Electricity and Tramways Committee to apply to the East Midlands Area Traffic Commissioners for Road Service licences, to run buses over the tram routes from Bailey Street to Dunstable Road and from London Road to Wardown, with an extension to Stockingstone Road. For this purpose, the Corporation had already purchased nine Daimler buses with both Duple and Willowbrook bodies – five single deckers and four double deckers. It was originally proposed, on 3 December 1931, to augment the Bailey Street – Dunstable Road service with buses and in fact to cut the trams back to two cars, running between the Town Hall and the Laundry. This was instead of the five or six cars required to cover the whole route. The original motorbus proposals of 31 November envisaged that nine buses be used on three new services, to compete with other bus operators, partly away from the tram routes. The three new routes were:

a) Park Street – George Street – Dunstable Road – Oakley Road and so on to the 'Sugar Loaf' at Leagrave using four double deckers on a twenty minute service.
b) Park Square – George Street – Cardiff Road – Ashburnham Road – Ferndale Road – Kingsway – Dunstable Road – Chaul End Lane, every thirty minutes using three single-deckers.
c) Park Street/Cutenhoe Road – Park Square – George Street – New Bedford Road – Alexandra Avenue – Biscot Mill with a thirty minutes frequency using two single-deckers.

However, it was decided on 15 December to apply for licences to substitute buses on all three tram routes. The addition of the Round Green route to the proposals was influenced by the fact that the Ministry of Transport was not likely to require the Council to repay the outstanding balance of over £11,000 of the tramway loan out of the ordinary course of three-yearly instalments.

Consequently, it was resolved to apply to the Ministry of Transport for sanction of a loan of £18,420 over an eight year period, to cover the cost of twelve buses in all (three more Daimler double-deckers for the Round Green route) and abandon the proposal to use the tramway reserve fund to buy the original nine buses. The fleet of twelve buses was insured for the sum of £286-4s-0d per annum.

After the Traffic Commissioners refused the Corporation's first Road Service Licence application on 1 December 1931, as a result of objections from six operators including the Eastern National, a further

application was made for the three proposed bus routes. This was granted on 18 January 1932 but did not include a proposed extension of the Dunstable Road route beyond the Depot to Cutenhoe Road, which even as late as the last week of February was still being included in the timetables. Altogether there were seven objectors with the Eastern National in particular wanting the right to run their buses through George Street.

One result of the Traffic Commissioners deliberations was that the Corporation was awarded exclusive use of George Street for their services. If this had not been the case the Eastern National would have got for nothing what they had earlier been prepared to purchase. The Corporation was also given the right to charge lower fares than Eastern National if they so desired.

Curiously enough, the first two routes to close on 28 February were the busiest and the least used, Dunstable Road and Wardown respectively. Consequently nine trams were towed by a *circa* 1914 Aveling & Porter traction engine (Regn No.5441) from the Depot into the adjacent Council dust destructor plant. It is not known which cars were involved apart from the fact that all of the top-covered cars were withdrawn from service (probably because they would foul the Old Bedford Road railway bridge) together with four other double-deckers and also No.13, the only single-decker. As only three cars were required to work the Round Green service, one of the remaining four was held in reserve at the Depot for emergencies. The four to remain were probably cars Nos.7, 8, 9 & 10.

The swan song of the Round Green route was short-lived, for on Saturday 16 April 1932, about seven weeks after the demise of the other services, the last car – open-top No.7 – ran into the Depot at 11.30pm, in pouring rain, unlamented and without any kind of ceremony, conducted by Mr George Webber. This was not unusual in those days; in fact some people were only too pleased to see the end of what they considered a most inflexible and unsuitable means of mass transport. That Luton's system could have aspired to any great glories is very doubtful, the narrow streets being unsuitable for successful tram operation.

Three other Municipal and one Company tramway, which had all survived for about the same length of time as Luton ceased operation in the early part of the year 1932. They were:-

ACCRINGTON	opened 1907
- closed 31 March	
BARROW IN FURNESS	opened 1904
- closed 5 April	
RAWTENSTALL	opened 1909
- closed 31 March	
WEMYSS & DISTRICT	opened 1905
- closed 31 January	
(A Balfour, Beatty Co.)	

Towards the end of this same year one other Municipal and two Company systems closed down:-

ROCHDALE	opened 1902
- closed 12 November	
MANSFIELD & DISTRICT	opened 1905
- closed 9 October	
(A Balfour, Beatty Co.)	

YORKSHIRE (West Riding)	opened 1904
- closed 25 July	

The Depot in Park Street was soon remodelled and the car shed became the new bus garage (it was subsequently relocated). A bus shed was built adjoining the north-east wall during the winter of 1933-34 which enabled the use of an earlier bus and coach operator's former premises (originally used by 'Blue Bird', now Wardown Garage) in New Bedford Road to be abandoned. A third shed was added to the NE side of the second building during the winter of 1935/6.

Though damaged in an air raid in September 1940, part of the car shed, complete with the foundation stone, remained inside the boundary of the Vauxhall car manufacturing plant. It was demolished a few years ago to make way for a car park. The foundation stone is now in the keeping of the Luton Museum authorities.

Not all the tram tracks were removed immediately, but those in the town centre, in George Street, were taken up in August 1932, when the whole road had to be closed for a month while the work went on! Many local residents were to be thankful for the tarred wood blocks recovered, thrown on their open fires during the following winter. All the cars taken out of service were offered for sale, but there were not any buyers forthcoming, even for the top covered cars, although some interest was shown by Bexley and Erith Councils. As both these undertakings were due to be taken over by the London Passenger Transport Board in 1933 the enquiries were probably a means of obtaining the market value of second-hand tramcars in connection with their own compulsory purchases! Other, more viable systems were already most probably better equipped than Luton. Eventually all twelve double-deckers were bought – it is said by Thomas Oakley & Co. (a local scrap metal dealer still in business) for £102 – to be offered for sale to private individuals and to thus go the way of many a proud electric tramcar – ending life as sheds, summer caravan dwellings, chicken coops and so on. Though this fate has often been described locally Thomas Oakley's son categorically states that it was not quite so. The negotiations were so protracted that they were eventually abandoned and T.W. Ward of Silvertown, London (part of the Geo. Cohen '600' Group) eventually bought the trams, which were cut up on site.

Before the last car disappeared from the Depot yard children used it for playing games. It is understood that one young boy fell from the top deck onto his head and died from the injuries sustained. After that incident the car was quickly removed. The fate of four of the cars at least is fairly well known. No.13, the car which had been used exclusively on the Wardown route for a long while stood in strange surroundings, used as a chicken house at Round Green. Car No.2 (top covered) met a sad fate. It was located by a group of local enthusiasts, truckless and used as a private dwelling, but otherwise in very good order – better than many at the National Tramway Museum at Crich, it has been said – in a field in the village of Streatley, north of Luton. They also had the option on a Brill 21E type truck and the owner of the body faithfully promised to let the group know when he wanted to dispose of it, when some suitable arrangement could be made. Some time passed and then it was learned that the body had been completely burned out! So disappeared any chance of rescuing and restoring that Luton car. Another car body stood for many years in a builder's yard in the St Mary's Street/Chapel Walk area of Dunstable.

Finally car No.6 survived as the office of an engineering firm in Tavistock Street, Dunstable – albeit only the lower deck – still painted in a shade of green, till the spring of 1973 when it was moved to a farm on the Bucks/Oxon borders. It was recovered from the farm by personnel of Luton Museum in April 1989 and now awaits restoration, under a tarpaulin, at Stockwood Country Park close to the M1 motorway. It is sitting on a Brill 21E truck. There is also a collection of wooden horse-drawn vehicles of all ages and a craft museum at this site. An Oporto (Portugal) single deck tram No.161 was bought from the Black Country Museum at Dudley in the West Midlands in 1990. The

body was put to use as a waiting room for the now defunct miniature railway which ran through the park. The tram was acquired principally for its truck, a Brill 21E which is an appropriate one for Luton No.6: Oporto 161 was a 'Brill 28' class tram and is from the first batch of twenty cars numbered 150 to 169, ordered from the J.G. Brill Company, Philadelphia in May 1912.

It has been stated elsewhere that old tramway rails were dumped on a rubbish tip in Bath Road in 1932. Seemingly they were used as reinforcement when the base of the Open Air Swimming Pool was cast on this site in 1935. Appropriately this road was at the end of the Wardown route, where the trams, if they had survived, would have been useful for carrying the many pleasure seekers. Some tram rails also still exist as edging to flower beds and paths in the gardens of some of the houses, up on the bank, on part of London Road near Ashton Road. There are also some in the possession of the Museum authorities, stored at Stockwood Park.

By 1980 the only evidence in the town to indicate there ever having been a tramway system were numerous overhead

side poles (see map) which were in use as lighting standards, many on roads which never saw a tramcar. During road improvements in Upper George Street near Christ Church in March 1969, some pieces of grooved girder tram rail were recovered and a short length of this, marked with the date 1907, the year when it was rolled, is now in the author's collection. Road improvements at the junction of Mill Street and New Bedford Road in 1970 also revealed evidence of tram tracks. The Wardown Museum established in the old house in Wardown Park has a few relics – timetables printed by Mr T.G. Hobbs (a local worthy of the Edwardian era) of 28 Cheapside, a few tickets of 1932 vintage and some Council records, along with a model of car No.2. Local enthusiasts, notably Mr Peter Hammond and Mr John Gilbert also have models of both double and single deck cars in their possession, which are displayed regularly on a sixteenth scale layout in the Transport Gallery of the Mossman Collection, at Stockwood Park.

The old *Saturday Telegraph* in its one time regular feature 'Saturday Parade' published photographs of Old Luton, and from time to time tramcar shots turned up which were avidly studied by the old folk who knew the trams well, and by some of the younger enthusiasts too, who were not so fortunate to have lived in the halcyon days of tramways. One last tenuous link with the tramways was severed in March of 1969 when the Electricity Works was closed down to make way for the town centre development. The Works have now been completely demolished.

Under the auspices of Mr Frank Hackett, one-time Curator of Luton Museum & Art Gallery, three tramway traction standards were rescued from High Town Road. They have been installed in Wardown Park and fitted with lamps to provide illumination in front of the Museum building.

It was speculated by a motorman interviewed in 1976, that a possible cause of the Midland Road accident was greasy rails. Normal practice, because it was a compulsory Board of Trade stop, was to apply the slipper track brake just after coming out of the curved High Town Road/Midland Road loop (it was not technically possible to do this sooner as the brake would get out of line with the rails, due to their curvature). If the car had started to run away on descending the hill a wheel brake application could lock the wheels on a greasy rail and the car would start to skid. Further heavy slipper brake application, a normal reaction, near the bottom of the hill, could result in lifting the car off the track. This could account for it carrying straight on instead of negotiating the curve. The fact that the car remained upright almost certainly indicates that the speed into the bend was not excessive, otherwise it is more likely to have been thrown over onto its side due to centrifugal force.

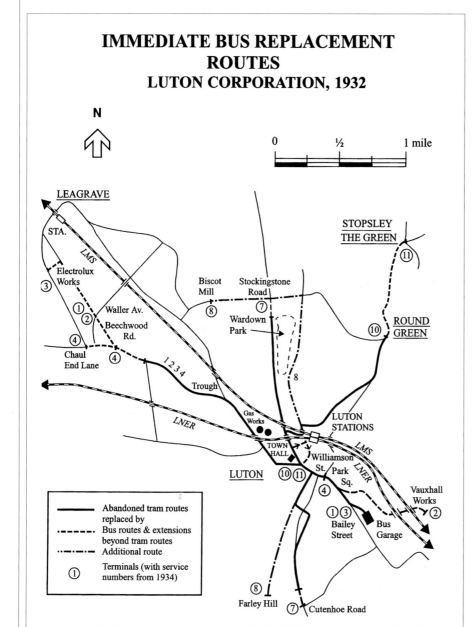

IMMEDIATE BUS REPLACEMENT ROUTES
LUTON CORPORATION, 1932

CHAPTER 6
ROLLING STOCK

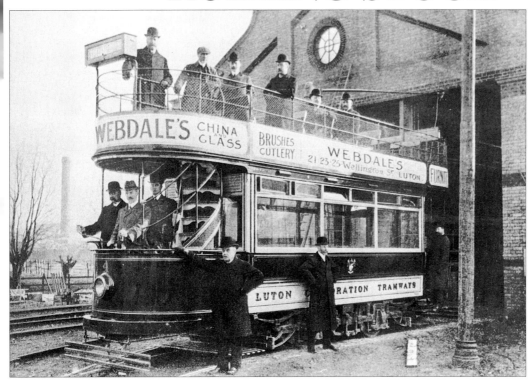

Bowler-hatted and moustachioed officials pose with newly assembled Car No.4 outside the Car Shed, 1908.

Twelve cars were delivered, probably by railway, for the commencement of operations, and finally assembled at the Depot. These were numbered – not unnaturally – 1 to 12, and were all non-vestibuled, open-top, double deckers, seating a total of 54 passengers, 22 inside the lower saloon and 32 on the top deck. They were mounted on 6ft.0in. wheelbase Brill type 21EM single trucks (i.e. four wheelers) supplied by Mountain & Gibson of Bury, Lancashire and were equipped with hand-operated wheelbrakes and Maley track brakes, as well as rheostatic electric brakes. The bodies were standard 'low bridge' height products, 27ft.6in. overall length by 7ft.0in. wide, built by the United Electric Car Company of Preston, Lancashire. Power was supplied at 500 volts to two 4-pole 30hp series wound motors. These, the control gear and other electrical equipment were of British Thomson-Houston design. Hudson and Bowring lifeguards were fitted and the half round collision fenders had provision for towing. The cars were equipped with four sand boxes and a gong, both items being operated by foot pedals from the platform.

The lower deck saloon had longitudinal polished wooden slatted seating and was fitted with three rectangular windows each side with two hinged ventilation lights over each window. These were arranged on some cars so that those at each end pivoted horizontally in order to scoop in fresh air, and the centre ones pivoted vertically. Above these were four tubular vents. The car roof was constructed of bent ash supports with a covering of tongued and grooved pine forming the upper deck flooring. The ceiling was veneered in three-ply maple and had oak mouldings. The

platforms were equipped with folding steps which nevertheless seem to have been kept unfolded in service. A semi-circular dash with a headlamp centrally placed was fitted to the platforms, from which the normal half-turn type staircases rose to the upper deck.

The upper deck extended over the platforms to form a balcony and had seven rows of reversible wooden 'garden' seats. These were double each side of the gangway, but with a single one alongside the centrally placed trolley standard, which had a swivelling trolley pole with a detachable head. The trolley pole did not have full 360 degree movement and therefore could only be swung one way. There was also a quarter round fixed seat at each end of the cars alongside the stairs. The 'decency boards' were fixed practically level with the tops of the seats and the sides were finished off with two rails above these with an infilling of wire mesh, to a height of 3ft.6in. Destination boxes were carried at each end above the upper deck top rail, illuminated at night by a single upright lamp inside a lamp bowl.

At a later date the destination indicators, originally roller blinds in glass fronted boxes, were altered in style when they were lowered to the level of the top of the safety rail, notably on cars 1, 2, 3, 10 and 11. From then on they appear to have been clip-on painted boards, apparently semi-permanently fixed, as it would seem that most of the cars were permanently allocated to a particular route. Photographs and written evidence indicate that cars 1-6 were used mainly on route A, 7-10 on route B and 11, 12 and later 13 on route C. These route designations were not official, but are a convenient way of differentiating them for the purposes of fare structures and so on; the

definition also changes over the years – see *Route Described* later in this chapter, and Chapter 7.

A dozen 16 candle power lamps provided illumination for the lower saloon of each car. An ordinary oil-lit tail lamp was hung over the rear dash. A 'FULL' indicator on a fold down flap was fitted under the canopy – just visible in photographs of No.10. There is, however, very little evidence of any widespread use of this device.

The only major modification to the original design was the fitting, in 1929, of cars 1, 2, 4 and 5 with curved top covers supplied by Brush Electrical Engineering Co. of Loughborough, Leicestershire. These were fitted with three vertically sliding windows in each side. The roof extended the full length of the car thereby forming a canopy over the balcony ends. As a consequence of fitting the top covers, the trolley poles were fitted to a trolley plank to one side of the roof of the car, in order to give adequate clearance under the low railway bridges. The single seats were also predisposed against the end bulkheads on the opposite side of the body to the stairs, alongside the sliding entrance doors. The trams with top covers were mainly used on the Dunstable Road route.

LIVERY
Livery was basically green and white (or ivory). The green has been described by ex-Tramways staff as 'moss green' and has been matched as near as possible by Mr John Gilbert and Mr Peter Hammond by scrapings from the remaining car No.6, as moss to British Standard 5-063. Dash, waist panels, decency boards, stair stringers and probably top deck rails were green, lined in white. Window and ventilator frames and rocker

panels were white. The dash, waist and rocker panels were lined out with a thin gold line with a thick black line on the outside, as were the staircase stringers and the risers to the stairs. At the corners of the panels the lining was carried out in the style known as 'Acanthus leaf' which was virtually the Preston standard. Emblazoned in the centre of the waist panels was the Corporation arms, surmounting the motto 'SCIENTIAE ET LABORI DETUR' ('May it be given to knowledge and industry') with the legend 'LUTON CORPORATION TRAMWAYS' in gold leaf shaded red filling the rocker panel. The fleet number was located just above the head-lamp and was six inches high. It was in gold leaf outlined in red and shaded in white and black. In early days there was an instruction on the canopy edge which read 'SWING THE POLE THIS WAY' with a suitable arrow. With subsequent repainting this useful reminder to platform staff appears to have been discontinued.

It would seem that in the very early days no advertisements were carried. Those that were subsequently added were, in the style of the times, mainly of enamelled iron. They were fixed to the ends and sides of the decency panels and advertised such well known national brands of goods as Robertsons jams, Bovril and Andrews Liver Salts. There were also local stores, shops and builders merchants, many of whom were still in business in the 1980s. They included B&C (Brentnall & Cleeland), Eastaffs, Evelings, Farmers Music Shop, Luton Co-Op, Merchants, Paris House, Stranges, Webdales and H. White bootmaker. An advertisement for 'Nubolic' soap was displayed on the backs of upper deck seats and risers of the stairs, about the time of the Great War. This must have been the most popular brand of soap of Edwardian times as it seems to have had a near monopoly of tramcar stairs on many

systems throughout the British Isles. Before the 'Nubolic' advertisement the risers were painted white in a sort of 'rosebud' pattern with the lower part green. After the War they were painted a plain dark colour. Various warning notices were painted on the rear of the stair risers, visible from the platforms. The most prominent being 'WAIT UNTIL THE CAR STOPS!' Translucent paper adverts also appeared on the ventilation lights and large posters advertising the latest films at the Palace Theatre, were stuck to the centre window of the lower saloon. Mr Walter Green of Luton was responsible for the handling of advertisements on the cars. At a later date, probably at the end of the Great War, most of the lining out, except that on the rocker panel, was discontinued. The roofs of the four cars fitted with top covers were most likely painted grey. It is also thought that the trucks of all the cars were painted Tuscan Red, at least in the early J.G. White and Balfour, Beatty days.

No.13 THE 'NEW TRAM' (Single deck – ex-Glasgow No 118)

No.13 was known locally as the 'new tram', arriving on the Luton scene some fifteen years after the original fleet. As described earlier, it was in fact much older than the other twelve, having been rebuilt and electrified in 1900/1903 by Glasgow Corporation, from a much earlier horse-drawn tramcar.

It was one of a batch numbered 1 to 120, rebuilt from the original double-deck horse cars (which were built between 1894 and 1898) as a stop-gap measure owing to a shortage of vehicles. They had open tops, a six window saloon with long canopies over-hanging the extended platforms and 90 degree turn stairs. There were seats for 32 passengers on the top deck and 18 in the

lower saloon. The six-feet long wheelbase, four wheel truck was a type 21E supplied by the J.G. Brill Co. of Philadelphia and was powered by two 30hp Westinghouse 49B motors. The type 210 controllers were likewise by Westinghouse and the cars were fitted with both hand and magnetic brakes. Before they were replaced in service by the new Standard Glasgow cars, between 1919 and 1923, four had already been sold to Dumbarton. Glasgow cut down No.92 to single deck in May 1910, seating 24 and it worked as a one-man operated car from Partick depot on the Finneston Street to Stobcross Ferry shuttle until 1925 when the route was abandoned. Later on it was used on the Paisley to Abbotsinch service from Renfrew depot, until withdrawn in 1938.

Car No.118 was one of the horse cars converted to electric operation which entered service from Possilpark depot as a Blue route car in 1903. It is one of the three double deck cars later converted to Parcels Cars (the others being 23 and 106) for an experimental service operating from St Vincent Place. Painted dull red with brown dashes, they only lasted for six months in parcels service. It then became a Ticket Box car supplying tickets to the various depots. No.118 was withdrawn in May 1920 and subsequently sold to Luton. At some time before it arrived, maybe even when it was a Parcels Car, it was fitted with two British Thompson-Houston GE52 30hp Motors and either B18 or 210 Westinghouse controllers.

The car was purchased from Glasgow on 21 May 1923 for £200 plus £50 for delivery. On entering service in Luton as No.13 it was used on the London Road-Wardown route, operating as a 'one-man' front exit car. Parcel shelves were removed and other modifications which were made on arrival at Luton cost the princely sum of £40. There were longitudinal seats for

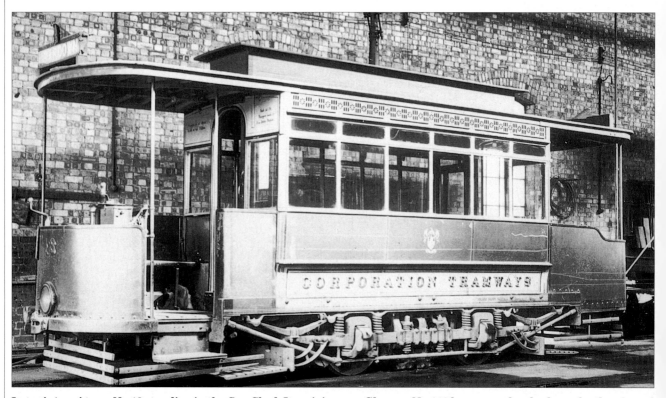

Luton's 'new' tram No.13 standing in the Car Shed. Its origin as ex-Glasgow No.118 horse car clearly shown by the pierced ventilators above the windows.

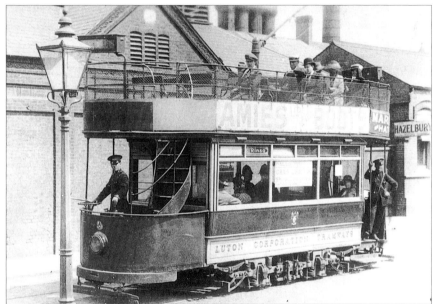

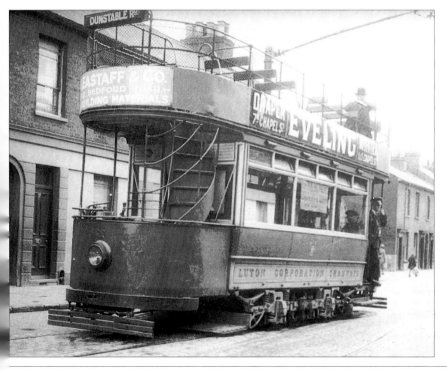

Top. **Car No.5, at the Round Green terminus it would seem, in the early days of the tramway.**

Middle. **Car No.9 at the Gas Works stop, en route to the Dunstable Road terminus. The precise date is unknown, though it is in the 'Corporation era' (that is, after 1923) with Conductor Mr. Jack Burley. Note two policeman riding inside.**

Bottom. **Car No.3 (in 'Corporation era') in Park Street having just left the Depot bound for Dunstable Road.**

eighteen passengers in the saloon and four seats were installed on the large platforms at each end. It is difficult to envisage it being overloaded except possibly in the fine summer weather when it would probably be replaced anyhow by a double decker. A clerestory, without lights, ran the length of the saloon and there were also glass fronted destination boxes fitted to the roof. The trolley standard was equipped with two external springs. Owing to the long overhang of the trolley pole, which obviated the use of a trolley rope, a long bamboo pole was carried in hooks attached to the truck frame. This was used for swinging the trolley pole at the termini.

The car was fitted with lifeguards, fenders and towing eyes at each end and a single headlight was mounted centrally low down on the dash just above the fender. A notice reading 'DANGER – FRONT EXIT CAR' was clipped over the dash at each end on the nearside of the vehicle.

It seems that the livery of No.13 was the same as the later unlined livery of the double deckers. The Corporation's coat of arms appeared on the waist panel, but owing to the shortness of the saloon it was found possible only to inscribe the lined out rocker panel with the words 'CORPORATION TRAMWAYS'.

A photograph in Mr Ian G. McM. Stewart's excellent book *The Glasgow Tramcar* shows No.118 running as a Parcels Car, still in double deck form but shorn of its upper deck seats. The photograph below it depicts No.92 as the one-man Finnieston-Stobcross Ferry shuttle. It will be noticed how similar is Luton's No.13 to this Glasgow car. It is suggested that Mr W.W. Clarke, the first Corporation Manager, might well have seen this conversion whilst visiting his family in Glasgow.

No evidence of any rail-mounted works vehicles has been discovered by the author, though the horse-drawn tower wagon mentioned earlier, employed during construction, may have stayed on afterwards. It is more likely however, that it was moved on to other J.G. White construction contracts. The 'smart little engine' reported in the press as smoothing out the points before the official opening may have been a portable rail-mounted rail-grinding trolley. Whatever form it took it too was probably passed on to subsequent J.G. White jobs, along with the tower wagon. The fact that no rail-grinding car was available could account for the deplorable state of some of the track in later years. It is of course possible to adapt a standard

Car No.6 on the Wardown-London Road route passing under the Midland Railway bridge in New Bedford Road; the Conductor is steadying the trolley pole by grasping back the trolley rope. Corporation operation, so post-1923.

car for rail grinding – just as was done to combat heavy snowfalls, by fitting a 'vee-shaped' snow plough. Abrasive blocks would be fitted to the centre of the truck and screwed down to bear down on the rails. The car would then be shuttled back and forth over the offending portion of track, or rail joint, until any corrugations were ironed out Of

necessity this work would have to be performed at night, or at least when no service was operating.

As a matter of interest, a much smaller system than Luton, the three miles long, 3ft.6in. gauge, single route Leamington & Warwick Tramways (a Balfour, Beatty company in later years) operated a works

car. In point of fact it was obtained second-hand from the 1½ mile single-route Taunton company and converted to a rail-grinder and general works car at Leamington. Subsequently it passed, in 1930, to the Llandudno & Colwyn Bay Electric Railway Co. Ltd (another concern associated with Balfour, Beatty). There it also served on

Car bound for Round Green, waiting on the Town Hall loop – note the diagonal cross bracing on the saloon bulkheads. The crew chat with an Inspector.

Unidentified Car, possibly No.10, entering the Depot yard – the gentleman with hat and pipe is part of the advert on the wall behind and is not sitting in the car!

works duties, until relegated for use as a store shed, in 1936.

Road surfaces in early tramway days were constructed of water-bound macadam which dried out and got extremely dusty. More sophisticated tramway systems than Luton's had electrically powered water sprinkler cars. These were used to spray the tracks, both to lay the dust and also to improve the electrical contact between wheels and rails, for the negative return current (the overhead wire being the positive). It must be presumed that the ordinary Highways Department horse-drawn water carts were used at Luton for this purpose.

A note about the history of the United Electric Car Co. Ltd.
This company was formed in 1905 by Dick, Kerr & Co. Ltd of Preston, Lancashire, by the amalgamation of its Electric Railway & Tramway Carriage Works Ltd (a subsidiary which it had formed in 1898) and the acquisition of the Castle Car Works (late G.F. Mines & Co. Ltd of Hadley, Salop, formerly of Birkenhead) and the British Electric Car Co. Ltd of Trafford Park, Manchester, for £85,000. Both these companies had gone into liquidation earlier, Milnes in August 1903 and BEC in the following year. This was due to a slowing down of the tramway building boom, consequent over-capacity in the tramcar building industry and a price cutting war between the five British manufacturers. Castle Car Works was formed by a syndicate of businessmen who bought G.F. Milnes and

BEC for £65,000 and subsequently resold it to UEC for £85,000.

An additional £15,000 was required by UEC for working capital and a 100,000 six per cent £1 preference share issue was put on the market on 1 July 1905. 75,000 shares were offered for sale to existing shareholders with the remainder being taken up at par by the Metropolitan Amalgamated Railway Carriage and Wagon Co. Ltd. From then onwards UEC concentrated all tramcar construction at its Preston works. After the formation of United Electric Car Co. Ltd there were just two other principal tramcar manufacturers left – Brush Electrical Engineering Co. Ltd of Loughborough, Leicestershire and Hurst, Nelson & Co. Ltd, Motherwell, Scotland.

UEC's parent company Dick, Kerr & Co. Ltd were already established as general engineers in Preston before the formation of its ER&TCW Ltd subsidiary. Subsequently, in 1918, the English Electric Co. Ltd was formed to take over and absorb Dick, Kerr, UEC and four electrical engineering concerns in Rugby, Coventry, Stafford and Bradford. Trams were built in many other towns, but many more were constructed (a total of 8,350) in Preston over the years than elsewhere in the British Isles.

THE ROUTES DESCRIBED
There were no route numbers used or carried on the cars, only destination blinds and, certainly in 1912, coloured headlights. So, for convenience, the routes will be called A, B and C. The destination blinds indicated

the main termini of each route, as did the headlights. These were as follows:-

A	PARK SQUARE – DUNSTABLE ROAD	White
B	TOWN HALL – ROUND GREEN	Green
C	LONDON ROAD – WARDOWN	Buff (quoted as yellow in 1910, probably looked buff colour due to age and dirt)

Also shown were:-
BAILEY STREET which was in fact the Depot
HIGH TOWN which appears to have been a short working on Route 'B' and
SPECIAL probably used for the Workmen's Dinner Car which ran on route A from Bailey Street to Leagrave Road.

It should be noted that two of the three routes passed through the town centre – George Street – and one started there and that all cars would have to traverse Park Street, Park Square and Market Hill into George Street in order to enter service.

The Depot was located behind the dwelling houses on the east side of, and parallel to, Park Street almost opposite the side street Bailey Street, which was the destination carried for the Depot. The cars left the Depot by a sharp reverse curve between houses Nos.149 and 151 and, once in Park Street itself, traversed a loop almost immediately. Continuing along Park Street towards the town centre, another loop was passed just before the junction of Lea Road near the *Black Bull* public house. A loop in Park Square served to form the in-town terminus of Route 'A'.

Route 'A' (Park Square – Dunstable Road)

Running in a generally north-westerly direction, this was by far the busiest of the three routes, serving as it did the working class area and the factory district. Leaving Park Square between stalls – where a street market was regularly held until February 1925 – the tracks negotiated a narrow curved section of Park Street and down the slight incline of Market Hill where the Ames Memorial, locally known as the 'pepper pot' and the Corn Exchange stood. At the foot of Market Hill, where George Street began, the tracks of route 'C', coming down Chapel Street joined. Immediately after the junction was a loop known as Cheapside loop. In a hundred yards or so, at the top of Bute Street, the line forked. Two legs of the 'Y' junction each had a loop, thereby giving the effect of a four track layout. This was the focal point of the system and was where transfers from one route to another took place. It was also a regulating point and a time clock was attached to the tramway standard between the diverging pairs of tracks. Route 'A' took the left hand fork up the rise of Upper George Street, which was very narrow, so narrow in fact that warning signs were erected stating 'NARROW SPACE BETWEEN TRAM AND KERB –DANGER'. At the start of Dunstable Road, between Inkerman Street and Cardigan Street, was the first of the five loops between there and the terminus at the Steam Laundry, near Kingsway. After passing under the Great Northern Railway Dunstable branch line, the second loop was reached by the Gas Works at Francis Street. There was another loop between Ivy Road

and Beech Road before the line forked left at the animal watering 'Trough' at the point where one of the proposed, but not constructed, extensions to Leagrave was intended to diverge. It is possible that a few yards of this proposed route, forming a spur into Leagrave Road, might have been built and used as a layover point for cars on short workings. Route 'A' then climbed the steep Beech Hill; at the top was the fourth loop, in Dunstable Road between Shaftesbury Road and Conway Road. From thereon it was but a short level run to the terminus, about a third of a mile away, just beyond Kingsway, with the last loop near Churchill Road. The total length of the route from Park Square was just about 1¾ miles.

Route 'B' (Town Hall – Round Green)

This route, of 1.3 miles, served High Town and Round Green, the north-eastern terminus lying about 550 feet above sea level. It started from the 'wrong' side of the loop in George Street at the Town Hall, close to the Public Library, which was endowed by the Scottish-American millionaire industrialist Andrew Carnegie, and left the town centre by way of Manchester Street. A longer than usual loop, of about 150 feet, was located between Bridge Street and Collingdon Street. After passing under the Great Northern Dunstable branch an acute right turn brought the tracks into the short length of Mill Street, where there was a loop by the *Royal Hotel*. A sharp zig-zag under the Midland Railway main line to London (scene of the worst accident) and up the steep rise of Midland Road brought the line to a loop on the curve and into High Town Road, in a north-easterly direction. This lengthy, narrow, road had a long loop from Cross Street to Havelock Road, through most of its shopping section, where the tracks ran close to the kerb. The lines continued along the rising High Town Road with a loop

at Jubilee Street, until at the top they joined Hitchin Road for a short climb to a final loop at Turners Knoll, a little way short of the terminus at Round Green. Here there once stood a much admired cherry tree, opposite the *Jolly Topers* Inn.

Route 'C' (London Road – Wardown)

This was the longest and most lightly used route, traversing as it did the more residential districts on each side of the town. It ran in a south to north direction, starting in the main London Road (the A6 that was) just south of a loop opposite Tennyson Road. Leaving this terminus, situated almost at the top of a steep hill, the line traversed a loop just before entering Ashton Road; at the bottom there was a sharp left turn at the *Hibbert Arms* into Hibbert Street. After crossing Castle Street the tracks formed a passing loop in Windsor Street before turning right into Chapel Street. Here there were two more loops, one between Elizabeth Street and Dumfries Street and the other opposite Stuart Street. On leaving Chapel Street by a left-hand turn the route joined the line from the Depot, in George Street. This route left the town centre where the Dunstable Road line diverged to the left of the Town Hall and followed Route 'B' along Manchester Street (where there was the long loop) and into New Bedford Road. It passed under two railway bridges before entering a loop alongside 'The Moor' public open space. A net was placed at the second bridge, which carried the Midland Railway, in order to prevent any falling railway telegraph wires fouling the tramway overhead wiring. The single track continued along New Bedford Road to the start of Wardown Park, where there was a loop at Lansdowne Road (the winter terminus in early days). It carried on for a further 500 yards or so to a loop just before the terminus at Wardown Lodge, opposite

Car No.11 at Town Hall loop in the late 'twenties, waiting to depart to Park Square, with the high wall surrounding the burned and vacant Town Hall site beyond. The figure appearing to hold up the trolley pole is in fact the statue on the War Memorial.

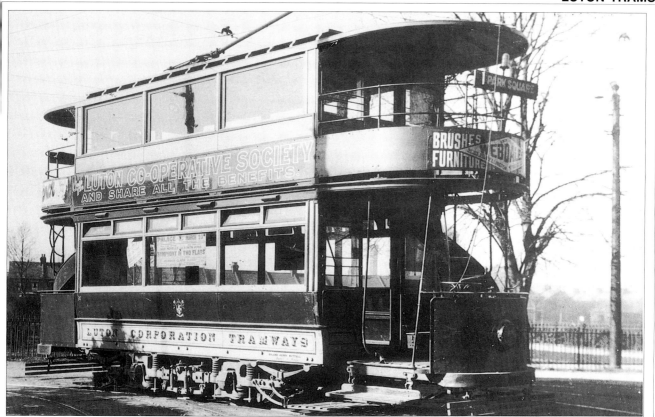

Car (No.1 or No.4) in the Depot yard.

Bath Road. The total length of this route was 2.2 miles. For readers who are familiar with the town it will be obvious that most of the loops were not within sighting distance of each other. Many of them were located on either side of bends or bridges.

It is believed that this arrangement of the three routes is correct, but it is interesting to note that the *Luton Year Book* gives different routes at different times. In 1907 it stated that the routes were:- Depot to Wardown Lodge; Depot to Dunstable Road and Round Green to London Road at the Borough Boundary via George Street and Chapel Street. In the 1912 issue it shows the routes as Bailey Street to Round Green; Park Square to the Laundry and London road to Wardown. In the following years of 1914, 1915 and 1916 the routes are described as Bailey Street to Wardown; Town Hall to Laundry and London Road to Round Green with the fare quoted as '1d for any distance'.

In 1925 the *Year Book* says that the routes are Park Square to Laundry; War Memorial to Round Green; to Wardown and to London Road, thereby suggesting four routes. It should be pointed out that the Laundry was the terminus in Dunstable Road, although it did not appear as such on the destination blinds. Also the War Memorial was, and is, situated at the Town Hall. A map in the 1913 *Luton News Almanack* states that the London Road route terminated at Trapps Lane, the former name for Cutenhoe Road and approximately 200 yards beyond Tennyson Road, but this was not so – the tracks never reached that far.

A proud crew pose with the slightly battered car No.10 on Midland Road/ High Town Road loop, on the Round Green route in the 1914/18 period – hence the lady Conductor. Note 'FULL' notice, folded away out of use

CHAPTER 7
TRAM SERVICES THROUGH THE YEARS
Bus Replacement Routes
Fares Structure and Tickets

Car No.4 standing in Park Street with destination blind showing High Town. The year is probably 1908 – no adverts on car side.

Dunstable Road Route

By July of 1910 the service frequency of this route was every ten minutes. In April 1912 the service varied between a ten minute workmen's service in the early morning and a fifteen minute interval until noon; thereafter the service ran every ten minutes. For the final hour, the cars again ran every fifteen minutes.

After the Great War this changed and by January 1920 this much-used route had a daily service with an eight minute interval. However, by April of that year, alternate Sunday journeys were running only between the Town Hall and Conway Road. Towards the end of the tenure of the lease things reached a pretty sorry state and by February 1921, Sunday services were withdrawn entirely.

When taken over by the Corporation in February 1923, the tramway services were rehabilitated and by September there was once again an eight minute daily service frequency. By 1930, the peak period headway from Park Square was four minutes and eight minutes off peak, but otherwise with only one car every forty minutes running the whole length of the route from Bailey Street (Depot) to the Laundry between the hours of 7am and 11.08pm and from noon on Sundays. By August odd short extra journeys were operated from the Town Hall to the Laundry.

Round Green Route

Up to July 1910 there was a daily ten minute interval service from the Depot. By April 1912 the interval varied between twelve and twenty minutes both on weekdays and Sundays. At some time, possibly towards the

end of the Great War, the town terminus was altered from the Depot to the Town Hall. January 1920 saw the daily interval fixed at thirteen minutes, and by April the Sunday services were changed from twenty-four to twelve minutes. As with the Dunstable Road route, Sunday services were withdrawn by February of 1921, and the weekday timing reverted to a thirteen minute interval. Weekday services were running every fifteen minutes by May 1921, and daily every fifteen minutes by February 1923. By April 1926 the daily service was every thirty minutes in the morning and every fifteen minutes in the afternoon. In 1930 an off peak service at fifteen minute intervals was provided by two cars from 7.15am, with an evening service of ten minute frequency, using three cars, until 11pm. With a headway of a quarter of an hour the Sunday service began at 2pm.

Wardown Route

A frequency as short as twelve minutes was operated on this route by July of 1910. Service frequency varied throughout the day between fifteen and thirty minutes by April 1912. By January 1920, the service was generally half-hourly. In April of that year the frequency was extended to 36 minutes with two weekday afternoon journeys terminating at Lansdowne Road.

In common with the other two routes, Sunday services were withdrawn by February of 1921 and the weekday intervals was twenty minutes. Further economies were made by May, with the weekday service extended to forty minutes and still no Sunday service. When the Corporation took over, the daily services were increased – to every

twenty minutes by September of 1923, but with the weekday morning frequency at forty minutes. By August of 1930 the daily service reverted to a twenty minute interval, from 8.30am to 10.30pm and from 2.30pm on Sundays.

IMMEDIATE BUS REPLACEMENT ROUTES AND SERVICES
Dunstable Road Route

The replacement for this tram route ran from the bus garage at Bailey Street to the junction of Beechwood Road, extended down Beechwood Road to its junction with Waller Avenue a distance of approximately half a mile beyond the original tram terminus. By the May of 1933 the basic weekday service was every twenty minutes and every forty minutes on Sundays, with additional weekday journeys to the Vauxhall Motor works. Short journeys were worked between Park Square and the junction of Beechwood Road and Dunstable Road, every seven or eight minutes, except on Saturday evenings when the frequency was reduced to five minutes. As in tramway days, there was no service on Sunday mornings. In April 1933 experiments were carried out with route numbering and from June 1934 new vehicles were equipped with number blinds. Route numbers were introduced in December 1933, as follows:

1	Bailey Street to Beechwood Road/ Waller Avenue.
2	Vauxhall Works to Beechwood Road/Waller Avenue.
3	Bailey Street to Electrolux Works.
4	Park Square to Beechwood Rd/ Dunstable Rd.

Nos.1 and 9 pass on the loop near the 'Trough' in Dunstable Road, sometime after 1929.

Route 4 was extended to Chaul End Lane, also about half a mile beyond the tram terminus, by July of 1935. Originally both the Works services, 2 and 3, which operated only at weekday peaks and lunch times, were restricted to employees of the respective companies. The traffic Commissioners lifted these restrictions on 24 March 1933 and the services were then made available to the general public.

Round Green Route
The route followed by the replacement buses differed slightly from that of the trams. It commenced just around the corner from the Town Hall tram terminus, in Williamson Street, and travelled along Manchester Street before turning into Bridge Street, but outwards initially via Mill Street instead of Bridge Street. From there it turned left into Guildford Street to regain the original route under the Midland Railway bridge, continuing on to the old tram terminus at Round Green. It was further extended some three quarters of a mile along Hitchin Road, to terminate at the village green at Stopsley, from the beginning of April 1933, after incorporation of Stopsley Parish within the Borough of Luton. On the inward journey to the town centre the buses ran along Guildford Street and turned right into Williamson Street in order to avoid reversing in George Street.

By May 1933 the weekday service was hourly to Stopsley and every twenty minutes to Round Green. During the peak periods and in the evenings, buses ran every half hour to Stopsley and every ten minutes to Round Green. The service to both Round Green and Stopsley was at fifty minute intervals on Sunday mornings, twenty minutes in the afternoon to Round Green and hourly (afternoons) and half-hourly (evenings) to Stopsley. In April 1933 the number 10 was allocated to the Round Green route and 11 to the Stopsley route.

Wardown Route
When the buses took over on 1 March 1932 they followed the tram route closely, though they were immediately extended at both ends. This only amounted to a few yards – to the corner of Cutenhoe Road at the southern end and, at the opposite end, an extension to Stockingstone Road of about 300 yards. The service was also an improvement on the previous trams as it ran every fifteen minutes. With the general numbering of routes in April 1933, this was given the number 7.

From 4 July 1933 a parallel service was run from Farley Hill to Stockingstone Road. This operated at thirty minute intervals at weekday peak periods, lunch times and evenings only and all day Saturday, but with no Sunday service. It was numbered 8 in August 1934 and diverted via Old Bedford Road and extended to Biscot Mill in March 1935.

Route numbers were originally experimentally introduced in April 1933, intended initially as a convenience for staff and Inspectors. This followed on from the acquisition by the Corporation of the ex-England's bus services. The route numbers were not generally advertised in public literature until 1 December 1933.

TRAMWAY FARES STRUCTURE
Up to 1911 the adult fares were 1d on each route, from the outer termini to the town centre, with a workman's return for the single fare. Towards the end of 1911 the single fares were increased to 1½d for the whole of each route with a child's single fare at 1d. By 1914 the fare had dropped to 1d throughout on all routes. Weekly workmen's tickets were issued at 6d for six days over any route. In 1926 fares were raised to 2d for the Town Hall – Round Green service with a 1d fare for children. Fares on the other two routes were 2½d for adults and 1½d for children.

1908-1911

A. PARK SQUARE to LAUNDRY	)
B. TOWN HALL to ROUND GREEN	) 1d adult
C. LONDON RD to LANSDOWNE RD/WARDOWN)	

March 1911

A. PARK SQUARE to LAUNDRY	) 1½d adult
B. DEPOT to ROUND GREEN	) 1d child
C. LONDON ROAD to WARDOWN	) 1½d workmen's returns

Workpeople's return tickets were available until 8.30am, between noon and 2pm and 5pm to 7pm. The stages covered by them were the same as the 1d and 1½d ordinary tickets. 1d Transfer tickets were issued between Bailey Street (Depot), Cowper Street, top of Collingdon Street, Villa Road and Havelock Road. Passengers transferring in George Street, at the Town Hall.

Oct 1911 to at least July 1913
A. PARK SQ to LEAGRAVE RD (The Trough)) 1d adult
TOWN HALL to CONWAY ROAD) 1d child return
CARDIFF ROAD to LAUNDRY)
B. BAILEY STREET (Depot) to CHARLES ST) 1d adult
TOWN HALL to WINCH STREET) 1d child return
MILL STREET to ROUND GREEN)

C. LONDON ROAD to CHEAPSIDE) 1d adult
COWPER STREET to VILLA ROAD) 1d child return
CHEAPSIDE to WARDOWN)

Also Depot journeys:
TOWN HALL to BAILEY STREET1d return

A. PARK STREET to LAUNDRY) 1½d adult
B. BAILEY ST (Depot) to ROUND GREEN)
CLONDON ROAD to WARDOWN) 1d child
Children under 12 same stages as Adult 1d single fare, 1d for return
journey

August 1914

In this month fares were reduced to 1d throughout on all routes. Half penny workmen's fares were available before 8am on weekdays, from 5pm to 7pm on Mondays to Fridays and from noon to 2pm on Saturdays, between the following stage points:-

A. BAILEY ST (Depot) to FRANCIS STREET (Gas Works)
FRANCIS STREET to LAUNDRY
B. TOWN HALL to WINCH STREET MILL STREET to ROUND GREEN
C. LONDON ROAD to CHEAPSIDE

Weekly workmen's fares at 6d for six days were available over any specified ordinary car route, outwards before 8.30am with return any time during the same day. Children's half penny tickets were available only over the same stages as the workmen's half penny tickets. Passengers parcels carried on the platform of the cars were charged at the rate of 1d each.

1926

By 1926 costs had increased and the fares charged were as follows:
A. BAILEY ST (Depot) to CHEAPSIDE)
LEAGRAVE RD (Trough) to LAUNDRY) 1d adult
B. HAVELOCK ROAD to ROUND GREEN)
C. LONDON ROAD to WINDSOR STREET) ½d child
MILL STREET to WARDOWN)

A. PARK SQUARE to WESTBOURNE ROAD)
TOWN HALL to LINCOLN ROAD)
GAS WORKS to LAUNDRY) 1½d adult
BAILEY STREET to GAS WORKS)
B. TOWN HALL to JUBILEE STREET) 1d child
MIDLAND RD (High Town) to ROUND GREEN)
C. TOWN HALL to LONDON ROAD) 1½d workmen's
HIBBERT ST (Castle St) to CROMWELL ROAD) return
TOWN HALL to WARDOWN)

A. PARK SQUARE to LINCOLN ROAD)
TOWN HALL to LAUNDRY) 2d adult
B. TOWN HALL to ROUND GREEN)
C. LONDON ROAD to CROMWELL HILL) 1d child
CASTLE STREET to WARDOWN)

A. PARK SQUARE to LAUNDRY) 2½d adult
B.-   -) 1½d child
C. LONDON ROAD to WARDOWN) 2½d workmen's return

Children under 5 years old were carried free. Those aged 5 to 14 years travelled an adult 1½d stage for a 1d, 2d stage for 1d and a 2½d stage for 1½d. Workers' passes (see *Rules and Regulations*) were charged 5d and dogs ½d, provided they were on the upper deck only and were carried at owner's risk. Also about this time a 1/3d weekly ticket was available entitling the holder to two single journeys daily except on Sundays. For four single journeys daily (excepting Sundays) a 2/6d weekly ticket could be obtained, either from the Inspectors or the Tramways Office on either Saturdays or Mondays, or from the conductors on Mondays only. Weekly tickets at half ordinary rates for Scholars were obtainable but only from Inspectors or the Tramways Office. The foregoing fares were probably in force for the remainder of the existence of the Tramways, until closure.

It is interesting to note that the early 1d ticket (1908-1911) shows fare stages London Road to Lansdowne Road on the Wardown route and it is a fact that the

winter services terminated at that point and not at the end of the track at West Lodge, Wardown Park opposite Bath Road. This practice was probably continued into the mid or late 1920s. Although Dunstable Road was always shown in the destination indicators on the cars, this terminus was usually printed as 'Laundry' on the tickets.

TICKETS

Only three tickets have come the author's way, although there are eleven examples in Luton Museum and Art Gallery from the later period after the Corporation had taken over. The three tickets in the author's collection are all from the Balfour, Beatty era. The earliest one (GC 3010) is from the years 1909 to 1911, a light blue 1d value when the fare was just one penny for the whole of each route. There is no printer's name on this specimen. The advertisement on the rear is: *'Wilson's is the best bread – Borough Model Machine Bakery – Luton'.*

The second ticket (B 0080) is a light buff (or white) 1d value. It is from the period 1911 to 1913 and is punched at Villa Road for a journey from Cowper Street on the Wardown (C) route. *'J W Green's noted Lutonian Ales and Stout – 1/4d per crate from Tenants and Agents only'* is advertised in red and black print on the reverse. This ticket was printed by Bell Punch Company of London.

The last of the three tickets (Cf 4870) is a 1½d Ordinary value deep blue, probably from the end of Balfour, Beatty's lease. It is punched at the Gas Works for a journey to the Laundry terminus of the Dunstable Road. *'GO TO Redrup and*

Open top Car No.10 and top covered No.2 pass on the Town Hall loop, after about 1929. Note diagonal body bracing on both cars.

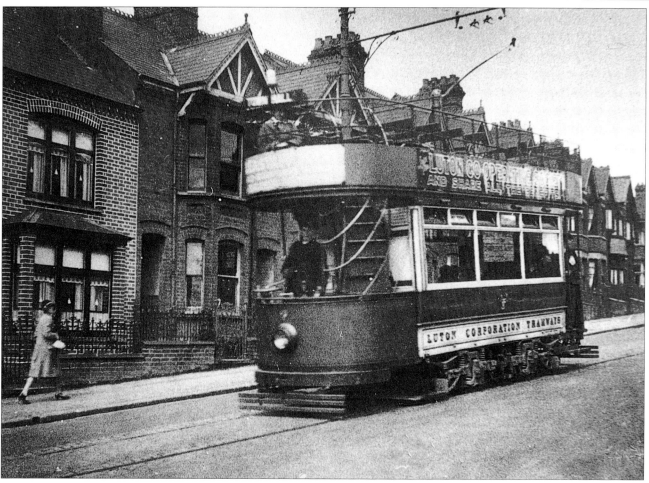

Car No.7 at Turners Knoll, after 1923, descending Hitchin Road on the Round Green route.

Car No.7, on the Town Hall loop, outside Sainsbury's and the Luton Building Society. Again the diagonal bracing rods are prominent across the end windows.

Very early days on the Luton tram, in George Street with the Town Hall in the distance beyond and the Cheapside loop and tracks to Park Street on right. On the left is the track to London Road.

Starkings Limited – Bakers, Grocers etc for Quality' is the advert on the back. Also printed by Bell Punch Co.

The above tickets are all headed *Luton Corporation Tramways, Balfour, Beatty & Co. Ltd, Lessees* – on three lines. The fare and conditions of issue are in the centre column and they are 'fully geographical'. The eleven tickets held by Luton Museum are dated 1932 and were probably donated about the time the tramways system closed. One of them (4026A) is a parcel ticket from Balfour, Beatty's time. It is a 1d value white, about 1¾in. square and was printed by Williamson, Ticket Printer of Ashton and is in fact more of a label than a ticket. All the passenger tickets, both Balfour, Beatty and Luton Corporation are the usual thin card and measure 1¼in. wide x 2½in. long.

A further four tickets are known to the author; one of them in particular being from the very first year of operation when J.G. White & Co. were lessees. This early example is Fa 2436, a 1½d blue, being the fare for a journey over each complete route – that is Bailey Street to Dunstable Road Terminus, London Road Terminus to Wardown Park, Bailey Street to Round Green Terminus – printed down the left hand side. The reverse of the above destinations are printed down the right hand side. The use of the designation 'Terminus' should be noted instead of the more familiar destinations of 'Laundry', Wardown, London Road and Round Green. This ticket is headed *LUTON CORPORATION TRAMWAYS – J G WHITE & Co. LESSEES* on two lines, immediately

below the number. The printer was Bell Punch Company, London and Uxbridge.

Ticket Sb 4041 is headed FARE – 1d – PS on three lines in the centre column. It is not clear what the initials PS stand for – possibly Park Square. From the early Balfour, Beatty period, it relates to journeys from Park Square to Westbourne Road, Town Hall to Conway Road, Gas Works to Laundry, down the left hand side. These destinations are all on route A. The journeys printed on the right hand side form the top are: Town Hall to Round Green (route B) Cheapside to Wardown, Town Hall to London Road, both on route C.

The two other tickets are from the Luton Corporation period. They are 1d ordinary, pink – Lo 3458 – a later version of No.2 below and Sn 4163 – a 2½d ordinary, light green, similar to No.5 below.

LUTON CORPORATION TICKETS
Of the remainder in the Museum, five are ordinary adult tickets, one is a half penny value Child, one a half penny Dog, and the other three are Workmen's Returns.

1. NL 9384 1d Ordinary Pale Cream
Probably from the period just after the take-over of the lease. It has thirteen stages down each side. The left-hand side has Town Hall six times and Park Square twice. The other stages are Gas Works, Midland Rd (High Town Road), Hibbert Street (Castle Street), London Road and Wardown. The base of the ticket has a blank strip without a printer's name.

2. Io 8997 1d Ordinary Pink
There are eight sections down each side, the lower three being blank. The stages are: Leagrave Road – Laundry, Bailey Street – Cheapside Loop, Havelock Road – Round Green, Windsor Street Loop – London Road, Mill Street – Wardown. The printer is Punch and Ticket Co. London N1. Period about 1926 – note use of the term 'Loop'.

3. Ht 9932 1½d Ordinary Bright Blue
Nine sections down each side. Stages are: Park Square – Westbourne Road, Town Hall – Lincoln Road, Gas Works – Laundry, Town Hall – Jubilee Street, Midland Road (High Town Road) – Round Green, Town Hall – London Road, Hibbert Street (Castle Street) – Cromwell Road, Town Hall – Wardown, Bailey Street – Gas Works.
Punch and Ticket Co. About 1926.

4. Xn 1637 2d Ordinary Yellow
Five sections down each side. Town Hall – Round Green, Town Hall – Laundry, Park Square – Lincoln Road, Wardown – Castle Street, Cromwell Road – London Road.
Punch and ticket Co. About 1926.

5. Sq 6715 2½d Ordinary Light Green
Two sections only down each side. Longitudinal printing facing outwards. Park Square – Laundry, London Road – Wardown. Blank strip at base without printer's name. About 1926.

6. Bj 9991 ½d Child Green
Apart from the colour of the paper, the printing is the same as ticket 2. (Io 8997).

7. D 0329 ½d Dog Green
Three sections down each side. Park Square –
Laundry, Town Hall – Round Green, London
Road – Wardown.
All the above tickets are headed Luton
Corporation Tramways in one line.

WORKMEN'S RETURN TICKETS
**F0312 1½d buff. Workmen's Return. WR
overprint Black**
Eight sections down each side. Park Square
– Westbourne Rd. Town Hall – Conway
Road, Gas Works – Laundry, Town Hall –
Jubilee Street, Midland Road (High Town
Road) – Round Green, London Road – Town
Hall, Hibbert Street (Castle Street) –
Cromwell Road, Town Hall – Wardown. The
WR overprint is longitudinal and reads from
the right hand side. Punch and Ticket Co.

**U 1996 2d Orange Workmen's Return. WR
overprint Red**
Five sections each side. This is the
Workmen's return equivalent of ticket
number 4 (Xn 1637). Although the stages
are the same they are arranged in a different
order, e.g. Town Hall – Laundry, Park Square
– Lincoln Road, Town Hall – Round Green,
London Road – Cromwell Road, Wardown
– Castle Street. The overprint is arranged
vertically W above R, blank base strip
without printer's name.

**I 3686 2½d Light Blue. Workmen's Return.
WR overprint Red**
This is the Workmen's Return equivalent of
ticket 5 (Sq 6715) with the stages arranged
in the same manner. However, Punch and
Ticket Co. appears at the base. The WR

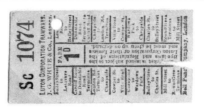

Top. 1d Fare. J.G. White & Co. Lessees
Middle. 1d Fare. Balford Beatty & Co. Ltd. Lessees.
Bottom. ½d Fare. Workman's B. B. & Co. Ltd.

overprint is longitudinal and reads from the
right hand side.

All three tickets above are from the 1926
period. Above the serial number is a row of
the initial letters of the six weekdays, which
would be punched in the appropriate space
for the day on which the ticket was issued.
Luton – Corporation Tramways is rendered
in two lines below the serial number. On all
ten tickets the conditions of issue are printed

longitudinally in the centre column and are
read from the right hand side. Although no
transfer tickets have come to light, they are
quoted in the Official Timetable, at least in
pre-war Balfour, Beatty days. Available at a
1d fare, with all transfers taking place in
George Street, they were for journeys between
any of the following points (Route letter in
brackets): Bailey Street (A), Cowper Street
(C), top of Colingdon Street (A), Villa Road
(C), Havelock Road (B).

The mourners seem to gather as the last of the tramway is torn up. These were the remains of the Cheapside loop in August 1932.

Removing the tram tracks in George Street, August 1932. The tie bars put in to maintain track gauge are clearly visible. Note stack of wood blocks.

On 30th August 1940 there were a whole series of complex engagements over southern England between the Royal Air Force and the Germans, and Biggin Hill itself was bombed. A substantial German formation was intercepted over Sheppey in the afternoon but nevertheless forced its way through as far as Luton, attacking the town and the airport as well as the Vauxhall factory and killing some fifty people. One of the casualties was the former Tram Shed, then in use as a bus depot (note the two single-deck buses).

List of Tramway Employees (incomplete)

Though nothing to do with the Luton Tramways *per se*, there is a document in the archives at County Hall relating to another 'tramway' – it was probably a railway siding from either the Great Northern or the Midland Railway. It states: *'We, the undersigned being five members of the Local Board of Health for the district of Luton in the County of Bedfordshire do hereby consent and agree that Messrs. Hayward, Tyler & Co. shall and may at their own expense make or construct a certain Tramway over and across a highway leading from Hitchin Road to the High Town Road in the said district of Luton which highway was formerly called Love Lane. The Tramway to be made upon a level with the Road and under the direction of the Surveyor of the said Local Board.*
As witness our hands and the Official Seal of the Local Board this 14th day of November 1871.
John Higgins, Chairman
Hugh G. ?
? Drewitt
? Barrett
Fred Davis
Countersigned George Bailey, Honorary Clerk to the Local Board.'

Mr. Ernest Price in his Inspector's uniform, in 1919.

G.W. Johnson	Depot Superintendent	1908
H.S. Butler	Cashier	1908
O. Hughes	Chief Inspector	1908
A.E. Horsler	Motorman (later Inspector)	1908
Geo.H. Aldridge	Motorman (later Inspector)	1908
William Raynor	Motorman (later Inspector)	1908
T. Rivers	Motorman (later Inspector)	1908
? Maycock	Motorman (later Inspector)	1908
? Duncombe	Inspector	1916
? Janes	Inspector	1916
Alfred Lloyd	Motorman	1916
C. Simpkins	Motorman	1916
? Hind	Motorman	1916
? Eaton	Conductor	1916
John Gunne	Motorman	1917
Thos. Wooldridge	Motorman	1917
Wm.H. Burgess	Motorman	1917
Wm.H. Saunders	Motorman	1917
Wm. Griffiths	Motorman	1917
? Lawrence	Motorman	1917
Harry Jennings	Inspector	1920
Fred Burr*	Motorman	1920
Ernest Shillingford	Motorman	1920
Ernest Price	Motorman (later Inspector)	1920
Ted Blackburn	Motorman	1920
Fred Buss*	Motorman	1920
Ken Thorn	Motorman	1920
E.G. Davis	Motorman	1920
Stan Perkins	Motorman (one-man car)	1920
Charles Wood	Motorman	1920
Jack Burley	Conductor	1920
Mrs E. Yorell	Conductress	1920
Arthur O'dell	Motorman	1920
? Clark	Motorman	1920
? Stokes	Motorman	1920
? Bradshaw	Motorman	1920
? Shillatoe	Motorman	1920
Jim Dransfield	Motorman	1926
George Webber	Conductor of last car (No.7)	

*same person?

Do you know of anybody else? Please let me know, via the publishers!

Some Rules and Regulations (during Balfour, Beatty's Lease)

Dogs not allowed inside cars

Holders of Workpeople's passes (obtainable at Tramway Offices) only can obtain Workpeople's Return tickets

1d and 1½d Workpeople's Return tickets (available until 8.30am, 12 to 2pm and 5 to 7pm) are issued. Stages covered by these are the same as 1d and 1½d Ordinary tickets (1911)

Children under 12 travel between same stages as Adults 1d fare for 1d return and 1½d fare for 1d single

1d Transfer tickets issued between the three routes. Between Bailey Street, Cowper Street, top of Collingdon Street, Villa Road and Havelock Road. Passengers to transfer in George Street.

Keep your tickets available for inspection

Tender the exact amount of your fare if possible

Passengers may ring – once only – to alight. WAIT UNTIL THE CAR STOPS

13 tickets for 1/- available for any 1d journey (Oct. 1911 at least until July 1913)

Smoking allowed only upon rear seats outside of Cars

Spitting is prohibited in or upon the Cars

Apply at Tramway offices for property left on Cars

Punctuality is striven for, but not guaranteed

The Town Hall clock is used for timing

Terms for Private Cars etc. on application

LUTON TRAMS

Please check the punch in your ticket when paying
Single tickets are only available on the Car issued
Passengers having personal luggage will be charged extra unless
it is carried by the passenger while on the Car
Additional Cars will be run as required
Please report complaints to the General Manager

A model tram posed on an uncovered fragment of track (the gentleman responsible standing over it in Brobdingnagian fashion) in Mill Street. The model is now in the Wardown Museum.

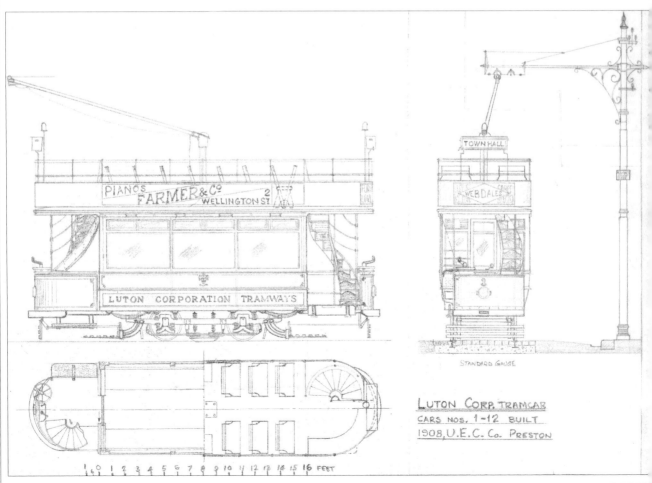

LUTON CORP. TRAMCAR
CARS NOS. 1-12 BUILT
1908, U.E.C. Co. PRESTON